Pelican Books
Private Police

Hilary Draper was born in Byfleet, Surrey, in 1954. She was educated at St Hilary's School, Sevenoaks, Kent, and studied law at Southampton University, where she obtained her honours degree, becoming a Bachelor of Laws. Called to the bar in 1976, she is now practising as a barrister in London. Hilary Draper first became interested in the subject-matter of this book at Southampton University, when she wrote a dissertation, as part of the degree course, on the law relating to private security firms, private detectives, and their activities. This is her first publication.

Hilary Draper

Private Police

Penguin Books

Penguin Books Ltd, Harmondsworth,
Middlesex, England
Penguin Books, 625 Madison Avenue,
New York, New York 10022, U.S.A.
Penguin Books Australia Ltd, Ringwood,
Victoria, Australia
Penguin Books Canada Ltd, 2801 John Street,
Markham, Ontario, Canada L3R 1B4
Penguin Books (N.Z.) Ltd, 182–190 Wairau Road,
Auckland 10, New Zealand

First published 1978

Copyright © Hilary Draper, 1978

All rights reserved

Made and printed in Great Britain by
Cox & Wyman Ltd, London, Reading and Fakenham
Set in Intertype Times

Except in the United States of America, this book is
sold subject to the condition that it shall not, by
way of trade or otherwise, be lent, re-sold, hired out,
or otherwise circulated without the publisher's prior
consent in any form of binding or cover other than
that in which it is published and without a similar
condition including this condition being imposed on
the subsequent purchaser

Contents

Acknowledgements

I would like to thank, firstly, Dr Albie Sachs, without whose help and encouragement this book would never have been written and, secondly, Superintendent Roy Barratt and Derek Engeham, who pointed me in the right direction at the start.

Of the numerous members of the security and detective professions, and others, who gave me assistance in my researches, it is impossible to mention everyone. I would most sincerely thank them all but, in particular, would like to acknowledge the help I received from the following: Vincent Carratu, Peter Cox, Philip Crofts, John J. Duffy, Norman Fowler, MP, Bruce George, MP. Peter Hamilton, Peter Heims, Fred Hudson, Anthony Kinghorn, Roy Monk, Tom Pescod, QPM, John Patoux, Charles Rice, Peter Smith, J. Philip-Sorensen and John Wheeler.

Introduction

The word 'police' is one that can be guaranteed to produce a reaction in most people, be it of trust, respect, resentment or ridicule. Add to it, however, the word 'private' and a somewhat different picture is conjured up; less defined but more sinister, less understood but more threatening. The purpose of this book is to attempt to remove some of the confusion and to discover whether there is any justification or explanation for the feelings evoked by the words 'private police'.

In its ordinary sense, the word 'police' refers to the civil body charged with the task of maintaining public order. The police to be examined here differ in that, although they often perform functions similar to those of the police proper, they are controlled by private enterprise working from a profit motive.

One reason for the confusion over the term 'private police' is not difficult to find. It is an everyday expression in North America and some European countries but there its significance is greater because the personnel of the security industry, due to licensing and the conferment of special powers, are much more closely associated with the official law-enforcement agencies, to the extent that in some countries they are auxiliary policemen. In England, 'private police' is a term used mainly by those who are concerned to awaken the public to the potential threat to liberty and privacy. You will never hear a representative of the industry itself in this country talking in terms of 'private police' or 'private armies', and this approach is in reality the more accurate because, as we shall see, the security guard and private detective generally have no more powers than the ordinary citizen and work within the confines of the law as it applies to you or me.

Let it not be thought, however, that the title of this book bears no relevance to its contents. The subject of private security is a vast and complex one, embracing every conceivable weapon of loss-prevention and detection, both mechanical and human. The advent of a new business specialist, the security consultant, bears witness to this fact. It would be wrong to write on this subject without touching on the fields of safe and lock, alarm systems, and fire prevention, which account for the business of many security firms. But as the title of this book suggests, my interest lies chiefly with the manned side of the security and private detective industries; the area of the watchman, the mobile patrol, the armoured-car guard and the investigator, which creates the nearest thing we have in this country to a private police force.

The civil police fall naturally into two sections, the uniformed 'copper on the beat' and the detective force. In the same way, the private sector of policing divides into the security-guard aspect and the investigative side of private detection. Space will also be devoted to some of the 'special squads' of the industry, for example, credit investigators, debt collectors and anti-terrorist organizations.

Although the broad division of the private security industry is easy to equate with that which is found within the police force, the two branches are very different, and are regarded by many as two totally separate and independent professions. I have found a tendency among representatives of security companies to dissociate themselves from private investigators, whereas the latter, particularly those involved in industrial investigation, like to be looked on as an integral part of the security industry. The question immediately arose, therefore, in the writing of this book, as to whether the two branches should be dealt with as completely separate topics or together, so far as practicable.

It is undoubtedly true that the security branch operates on a far larger scale than that of detection and constitutes a modern and rapidly expanding industry; nevertheless I decided in favour of the second approach for two main reasons. Firstly, there is some degree of overlap between the security and investigative professions, with detective agencies beginning to expand into security services, and the smaller security firms offering investigations as well. Secondly, and more important, it is convenient to deal with the security and detective branches together because of the many common problems posed and faced by them. For example, both are concerned with the question of control over the personnel employed in their respective industries and, as we shall see, in several countries this has been solved by a compulsory licensing system for private detectives and security guards being combined in one statute.

The state of the security and detective industries and their role in society today should be a matter for concern and for closer examination; concern about the private detective because, as the Younger Committee Report on Privacy pointed out, the invasion of privacy is the essence of his work; concern about the security firms because the rapid escalation in the number of serious crimes has made their industry one of the fastest growing this decade; and concern about both because their work by its very nature provides for access to industrial premises, cash and high-value goods, and confidential information.

This book does not purport to cover all the many aspects of the subject 'private police', far less is it intended to be a textbook on the theory or technology of security. What it does attempt to do is to convey a picture of private policing and investigation in this country, a picture formed not from within the industry itself, nor through the eyes of an over-imaginative or sensational film director, but from the point of view of the layman – the 'woman in the street' – looking, it is hoped, objectively at the achievements and shortcomings of an industry that has almost overnight forced its way into a significant place in modern society.

1. In the Beginning

There is very little written about the history of private security, and it is difficult to trace the exact origins of this profession of protection and detection. Mention of bodyguards, watchmen and spies can be found in the earliest documents throughout history, although it is necessary to look to the nineteenth century to see the beginnings of security in the organized commercial form that we recognize today.

So far as private detectives are concerned, the very first recorded case of an individual spying on another for gain dates back to the time of the Phoenicians, when someone obtained information for a member of the royal household that his wife was consorting with the leader of the army. Then there were the Biblical spies such as Joshua and his eleven companions who were sent out by Moses to spy on the people of Canaan. There have been similar reports of spies at work throughout history, mostly in a political or military context, but there were privately hired spies too, usually centred around the royal courts. Lord Walsingham, a minister during the reign of Queen Elizabeth I, created the largest network of spies in Europe, and their efficiency in uncovering the plots of Mary, Queen of Scots, and others is proven. The next century saw Cardinal Richelieu of France at the centre of a web of intrigue which made it essential for him to know exactly what was going on around him. So he paid spies to keep him informed of the latest developments in the 'affairs of Court'.

It was not until 1817, however, that private detection took shape as an organized profession under the guidance of a Frenchman named François Eugène Vidocq. Pinkerton may well be the most famous factual private detective of all time and be thought of as the pioneer of that profession, but although he provided the origins for the expression 'private eye', he was not the first. He was preceded by a matter of thirteen years by Vidocq, who established an investigation bureau in Paris and achieved some notoriety by publishing his memoirs, thus becoming the first writer of detective stories.

Allan Pinkerton, the Glaswegian who emigrated to America, was not long in following and in 1830 established the forerunner of the largest detective agency in the world. He specialized in criminal investigation and was responsible for tracking down some of the most dangerous outlaws of the day. His exploits have inspired many books and films, including *Butch Cassidy and the Sundance Kid*. The Pinkerton files on known criminals were the first of their kind, and were used by the official law-enforcement agencies for many years until the FBI established its own files. In an age where corruption among the police was at a peak, the Pinkerton men had a reputation for integrity, but the agency lost a great deal of public respect when it began to accept political assignments and strike-breaking jobs which culminated in a battle at the Carnegie Company resulting in the deaths of nine Pinkerton men and eleven workers. Pinkertons has since returned to its former glory, however, and now constitutes one of the largest security and investigative organizations in the United States, and in the world.

In England private-detective agencies began to spring up around the middle of the nineteenth century, but it is difficult to associate them with the Pinkerton Agency in America because the nature of their work was so different. It is interesting to discover that the private-detective profession in this country was in fact an offshoot of the other branch of the industry through the security agencies that were in existence at the time. These small organizations, as will be seen later, supplied men to guard houses, factories and other premises at a time when crime went almost unchecked.

It was the Matrimonial Causes Act of 1857 which paved the way for these agencies to branch out into the field of detective work, and as the title of the statute suggests this, at first, took the form almost exclusively of divorce enquiries. Divorce at this time was definitely a pursuit of the rich; the huge cost of legal fees ensured this fact. But for those who did have the means, there grew up a band of enquiry agents ready to find evidence, often at any cost, for the prospective petitioner.

These first private detectives did not always confine them-selves to the collection of divorce evidence; they often expanded into related areas of work. Many agencies, for example, supplied prostitutes as well as enquiry agents, and the situation led to the idea of 'hotel evidence' – the practice of providing, at a price, a woman to be seen with a gentleman client in a hotel, where he would be conveniently 'spotted' by an enquiry agent.

Other detectives did not stop at fabricating evidence. At a time when divorce costs were at a premium, mistresses were numerous. It was the age of clandestine meetings and secluded apartments, and enquiry agents stepped in to fulfil a widespread need for 'mistress-managing' – the renting of apartments and the arranging of meetings. The drawback was that private de-tectives thus became the possessors of highly confidential and potentially ruinous information, and some did not hesitate, at a later stage, to use this knowledge for the benefit of the other side and give evidence on behalf of the wronged spouse. Harry Benson was a well-known Victorian 'private eye' who used his investigative powers to uncover scandals among prominent people and the aristocracy, and then blackmailed their families into paying for his silence.

As the demand for divorce enquiries grew, so private-detec-tive agencies began to develop independently of the security agencies from which they had first emerged. They started to look around for other areas into which to expand, and before long recognized a ready market for their services in the in-dustrialists who were facing increasing problems of unrest and political activity among their workers. Agencies, therefore, offered to hire out men to infiltrate factories and workmen's social clubs in order to detect cases of strike-making and inform on the ringleaders. This sort of work was bound to increase the unpopularity of the private detective; indeed one agency well known for its industrial activities was burnt to the ground by enraged workers.

Towards the end of the Victorian era, the free rein that these disreputable detectives had enjoyed began to tighten. The police started to take a less benevolent view of the practices of black-mail and deception which were allowing many an agency chief to live in comparative luxury. Furthermore, the courts began to reject the evidence of private detectives in relation to matri-monial affairs, in situations where it had previously been ac-cepted, when it appeared too coincidental or contrived. The scope for the use of lies and false evidence in the divorce market was disappearing. In 1901, Garnier's detective agency was founded and became one of the first multi-purpose firms, offering all kinds of investigation services. Others followed suit, and this became the pattern of the twentieth-century agency; the Victorian enquiry agent had matured into the modern private detective.

Meanwhile, at about the time that detective agencies in this country were beginning to establish themselves in their own right, men on the other side of the Atlantic were laying the foundations of the modern security company. It was in the year 1850 that a man named Henry Wells founded the American Express Company, the same year that Pinkerton expanded into guard services with the Protective Patrol. Although Wells was not strictly the first 'express man', it was he, together with Wil-liam G. Fargo, who joined him in 1852, and Alvin Adams, who organized the Adams Express Company in 1854, who pioneered the art of security transport. The company Wells Fargo became a legend in American history, and the running of a nineteenth-century security firm was portrayed to millions through the television programme of the same name. Even now the words 'Wells Fargo' conjure up a picture of stage coach and armed outriders, rather than the armoured vehicles that can be seen bearing the name of that original company on American streets today. Another of the largest cash-carrying firms in the United States, Brinks Incorporated, can trace its roots back to 1859 when Perry Brinks took advantage of the demand for secure transportation of goods to start his own company; and 1858 saw the beginning of the alarm company when a man named Edwin Holmes set up the first central office burglar-alarm operation.

It can be seen that the early history of the security company as we know it today belongs to America. Its development, well ahead of European counterparts, can be explained by the spreading towns and migrating population which characterized the United States at this time. In England and the rest of Europe, a community existence remained which, together with poor communication, prevented the need for security transport companies until almost a hundred years later.

That is not to say that there was no form of private security in this country until the twentieth century. On the contrary, it was as early as the sixteenth century that men were first paid by private individuals to watch over private property and to keep the peace generally. This situation came about by reason of the system of 'watch and ward' which was laid down by the Statute of Westminster in 1285, by which a watch had to be stationed in every town. The watch was supposed to be made up of men of the town who worked on a rota basis, performing the duty for about a year, although they were unpaid. By the sixteenth century, the wealthier tradesmen and townsfolk had become reluctant to take their turn, and so developed the practice of paying 'deputies' to serve in their place. Because these deputies also began to delegate the job, it eventually fell to the otherwise unemployable to fill the position of watchmen, and thus it was that Henry Fielding was later to say of these 'Charlies', as they came to be known, 'They are chosen out of those poor decrepit people who are from their want of bodily strength rendered incapable of getting a living by work. These men armed only with a pole which some are scarcely able to lift, are to secure the persons and houses of His Majesty's subjects from the attacks of young, bold, stout, desperate and well-armed villains.' Thus the private security industry did not get off to a particularly auspicious start.

Due to the collapse of the watchman system, private guard forces began to develop in a different way. As the old machinery for keeping law and order broke down, so crime flourished and increased with almost no opposition or control. Within London, parts of the city became havens for thieves and footpads, while outside the towns, the countryside was haunted by highwaymen, which made travelling by coach a risky business. Eventually the stage-coach companies and private owners tried to overcome the threat by carrying guards on their vehicles, but the heavy blunderbusses with which many of them were armed were too cumbersome to be effective.

In London itself, the wealthy merchants in the City hired retainers to watch over their premises and keep the elegant squares in which they resided free from trouble. These private guard forces were made up of much more suitable men than those who constituted the watch; they were younger, stronger, armed with staves and pistols and sometimes muskets for use in emergencies. But while these small pockets of rich merchants remained relatively peaceful, the rest of London was barely safe to walk through. Efforts were being made to improve the situation. The Fielding brothers, Henry and John, successive Chief Magistrates of Bow Street, campaigned fervently for reform of the watchman system, and sowed the seeds of origin of the Bow Street Runners with their bands of 'pursuers', who were paid for out of a grant from the Treasury.

Attempts by the Fielding brothers and later by another magistrate, Patrick Colquhoun, to persuade the Government to legislate in this area failed however. It was Colquhoun who, frustrated in his efforts to reform the policing system in the capital, turned his attention to the Port of London around which a large proportion of the crime was centred and where it was estimated £$\frac{1}{2}$ million was lost annually through theft and pilferage. Here he set up the Marine Police Establishment in June 1798, a body which must be regarded as one of the first organized private police forces, since four-fifths of the expense of running it was undertaken by the West Indian merchants who operated in the Port. The Establishment employed sixty officers and achieved such success within a short period of time that in 1800 these river police became a public body.

Within thirty years of this event the Metropolitan Police was formed but the need for private forces did not die out. There was no chance that the newly organized London police force could rid the City of over 100,000 habitual criminals overnight. The demand for guards to watch over private premises continued and was met by the security agencies which had opened all over London to answer the call for preventive forces. They provided watchmen for factories, offices, large houses, warehouses and other premises, and supplied personnel to keep an eye on valuables – in particular at large private functions where there were bound to be many wealthy guests. Gradually, however, the new police force began to bring the crime situation under control and the need for private guards diminished. The security agencies turned to detection as well as prevention, and eventually enquiry work superseded their original function.

It was at about this time – the middle of the nineteenth century – that Wells, Fargo and friends were beginning to combine transport and security on the other side of the Atlantic, but it is necessary to jump a hundred years to get the next glimpse of private security in England, and the first glimpse of it in corporate as opposed to individual form.

It is commonly thought that 1935 was the year which saw the beginnings of the security company in this country, with the formation of Night Watch Services, the forerunner of the giant Securicor company. In fact the origins can be traced back nine years, to 1926, when a man named Arnold Kunzler founded Machinery and Technical Transport; the word 'technical' in reality stood for 'security', but the company believed then (as it believes to this day) that one of the secrets of security is anonymity. As is apparent from its name, Machinery and Technical Transport (which later became MAT Transport) specialized in the carriage of goods, including cash and valuables. The company's first bullion job is shown in the records as having been undertaken on 29 March 1926. In these early days, this service was performed by couriers who accompanied loads by road, rail or air to their destinations. It was not until much later that the idea of special security vehicles was adopted.

Night Watch Services (alias Securicor), however, can claim to be the precursor of the modern guard company in England. It was formed by the Marquis of Willingdon and Henry Tiarks, a merchant banker, and began by employing fifteen uniformed guards to patrol Mayfair homes whose proprietors were away. These watchmen rode bicycles and carried truncheons and whistles to summon help if necessary. After a lull during the war years, the company revived, but this time only a 'static guard' service was offered. Gradually the company extended into the industrial field, guarding factories and business premises.

The next important date in the history of manned security is

1955. This was the year that Roy Winkelman formed the Armoured Car Company, which was modelled on the large American cash-transport companies, Brinks Inc. and Wells Fargo. Five years earlier, Winkelman's foresight had enabled him to recognize the possibilities of such a company in this country. He was thus encouraged to go to the United States where he worked for Brinks, and so gained the necessary 'know-how' to start his own company in England. The armoured vehicles themselves, which grew in number to become a fleet of over 100, were modelled, internally at least, on those of the American Brinks Inc. However, Winkelman modified the external appearance of the armoured cars to look as much like ordinary commercial vehicles as possible. The reason for this was that security companies in general were already the target of attack and opposition from politicians and others who accused them of constituting a second police force, a private army; Winkelman certainly wanted to avoid, if at all possible, the appearance of being the 'tank corps'.

The Armoured Car Company was the only one of its kind in this country for many years. Securicor, which in 1960 had been taken over by the Kensington Palace Hotels Group under Keith Erskine, was anxious to expand into the cash-carrying market, and looked to the Armoured Car Company for the means. But Winkelman did not wish to sell to Erskine and the giant Securicor organization. Instead he negotiated a sale with Chubb, the lock and safe people, but was defeated in the end because Chubb promptly resold the company to Securicor.

The security industry had begun to hit the big time in this country. In the same year that Securicor was taken over by Kensington Palace Hotels, the De La Rue organization formed its subsidiary, Security Express; and Group 4 Total Security (formerly Factoryguards), of Swedish parentage, expanded its operations from the North-West of England into London. To this day, these three companies constitute the 'Big Three' in this country on the guarding side of security, although other large companies have entered the arena, including the Chubb organization with its Chubb Wardens and several big American firms who have expanded into the British market.

In looking at the development of private security in this

country, it is necessary to mention a special body of police who fall between the commercial guarding firms and the regular police force. The chief members of this group are the dockyard and transport police. They, together with certain other miscellaneous forces, are raised by the public or semi-public organizations in question for the specific purpose of guarding their property and enforcing their by-laws. The docklands used to be policed by off-duty regular policemen, but when this became no longer possible, the port authorities started their own police forces. At the time of writing, Manchester, Belfast, Southampton, Dover, Port of Bristol, Port of London and Merseyside all have their own police forces, the last mentioned having been formed only in the last few years. In constitution the Docks Police are similar to the British Transport Police employed on the railway and Underground networks. To all appearances they have the same powers of search and arrest as regular police, the only limitation on these powers being in terms of the area in which they can be exercised. In most cases these police are restricted to operating within the area controlled by their employers. In some cases, however, for example the Mersey Docks and Harbour Police and the Port of London Police, that area is extended to within a mile outside the boundaries of the docklands – an extension that can prove invaluable to the security forces.

These special private police bodies work in close liaison with the police force. In 1971 their numbers were estimated by Peter Hamilton and W. E. Randall in a paper 'The Security Industry of the United Kingdom' at 15,159, although this number also included the constabularies of the Armed Forces and investigation services of the Board of Trade, Post Office and Customs and Excise departments.

Although Docks and Railway police are in a sense private police forces they do not fall within the scope of this book which relates chiefly to the work of commercially run security and detective firms. Similarly it would be impossible to cover the whole range of security personnel in this country who subsist independently of those firms. There are the thousands of men, predominantly ex-policemen or fire-service men, who are employed directly by industry, as opposed to being under contract from a security company. Most hotels, department stores, factories, office blocks and other large premises employ one or more permanent security officers to supervise the protection of the building from fire or crime. Large concerns requiring especially tight security such as art galleries and law courts will employ a small army of permanent staff for security duties. Many of their duties and activities are similar if not identical to those of the commercial security guard on internal guard work. Many of the problems created and faced by the security industry are commonly shared by these 'in-house' guards. Therefore much of what is said in this book, particularly in relation to licensing and control, will apply equally to these individual security personnel as to their corporate counterparts. But it is not within the scope of this book to examine in detail their function.

Having thus traced the history of private detection and security up to the present, and examined briefly some of the fringe elements of the industry, it is necessary to consider the state of the industry today in order to appreciate some of the problems that have resulted and to understand the reasons for the concern about the industry that exists in some quarters.

As far as private detectives are concerned, there is nobody who knows precisely how many are operating in this country. On the contrary, estimates have varied from 1,000 to 20,000. In 1972 the Committee on Privacy, chaired by Sir Kenneth Younger, accepted 3,000 as being the most likely number, but it is hard to imagine how this figure was arrived at when there is no register of private detectives, and no indication is given as to whether this includes part-time as well as full-time investigators. A further difficulty in establishing the number of private detectives is created by the fact that most of them rely almost entirely on solicitors' practices for their work and therefore have no need to advertise to the general public; many operate from their own homes and give no outward indication of the nature of their profession.

There is a similar problem in trying to ascertain the number of security companies. Apart from those which are almost household names, there are literally hundreds of smaller firms operating through the country. In 1973, the Secretary of State for the Home Department put the figure at 741 (including those companies installing security equipment) and as the industry is one of the fastest growing – with an annual expansion rate of about 15 per cent – it can be assumed that this number has increased substantially since then. The reason for the comparative prosperity of the security world at a time when the rest of industry is in recession is due mainly to the ever-increasing crime rate, although some credit is also due to the insurance companies which are demanding higher security standards from policy holders. It should not however be assumed that all firms venturing into the security field are automatically successful. A large amount of the growth rate is absorbed by the large companies, and there is quite a high incidence of change in the identity of those firms making up the remainder of the industry. A firm might go out of business one day and its place be taken by another the next; mergers and takeovers of smaller outfits are also common. The number of security companies is therefore never a constant one, though the general direction is towards an increase rather than a decrease.

In 1971 it was estimated, in the paper presented to the Cropwood Conference by W. E. Randall and Peter Hamilton, that in the whole of the United Kingdom there were approximately 105,000 private policemen (including those employed by the public bodies mentioned above, but excluding private detectives) as opposed to about 110,000 public police. In 1972 *The Times* of 19 August reported a member of the Police Federation as saying there were as many uniformed security men in Britain as there were policemen. Today the numbers of regular police officers in the United Kingdom total nearly 128,000. With the police force in England alone 8,000 men understrength, and a growth rate in the private sector, as we have seen, of 15 per cent, it must now be true that private security personnel possess superiority in numbers. Securicor, by itself, accounts for more than 20,000 of these, and Group 4 for 4,000, while Security Express are the third largest in the guarding field. In addition there are many firms employing a significant number of men in the middle range of security operations. Some companies elect to limit expansion to a field with which they are familiar, expending energy on improving techniques in that field. Others extend their operations into new and sometimes ancillary areas wherever there is a demand. Size is not, of course, synonymous with security; indeed there is a possibility of expansion leading to a slackness in the selection of staff or a loss of control from the centre, a danger which the largest firms are very aware of, and attempt to guard against.

Thus we come to possibly the most important feature of the state of the security industry in this country today. In a profession which is concerned with the detection and prevention of crime, there are absolutely no restrictions in law on who may set up in business as a private detective or a security firm. He need have no particular training and no experience; there is nothing to stop even a convicted criminal from entering the security industry. The only standards in operation, as we shall see, are those imposed voluntarily by firms or associations.

There are several associations in existence whose aim is to promote a better image for their members and establish standards in the industry. On the detective side, there is the Association of British Investigators (ABI), which can trace its origins back to the year 1913 and boasts one of the largest memberships of any detective organization in the world; and also the Institute of Professional Investigators (IPI), a new organization chiefly concerned with raising academic and business standards among investigators. On the security side, the British Security Industry Association (BSIA) and the National Supervisory Council for Intruder Alarms (NSCIA) are the two associations which confine their energies to improving standards among security and alarm companies, while the International Professional Security Association (IPSA), formally the Industrial Police and Security Association, spreads a wider, if slacker, net over the industry, catering for individuals rather than companies. The standards and effectiveness of these organizations will be examined later; suffice it to say at this stage that they are the only standards among private detectives and security firms in operation at the moment.

The nature of the work undertaken by private detectives and security firms has been changing over the last decade, and the fields in which they operate extended. These will be examined, along with their methods and practices, both legal and illegal. But the question that has to be asked is whether the law has kept pace with the developments. Would Monsieur François Vidocq and Mr Henry Wells, the initiators of modern detection and security respectively, be content with the present state in this country of the industry to which they gave commercial viability?

2. From Adultery . . .

The private detective is much more the product of the American film industry than a three-dimensional character. Try as they might, reputable firms of private investigators have not yet succeeded in shaking off the Hollywood image of a glamorous and exciting life spent tracking down murderers and missing death by inches. They still receive frequent job applications from those with visions of becoming a second Sherlock Holmes or Philip Marlowe. As one investigator said to me, 'You can spot them a mile off because they put things like "Karate" and "Art of Disguise" in the hobbies section of the application form.'

At the other end of public reaction is the private detective's reputation as a sordid snooper; the man in the dirty raincoat with upturned collar, watching lights go off in bedrooms and storming in with camera and flashbulb at the ready.

Security guards, on the other hand, are very far removed from the glamour of the cinema screen. In their capacity as valuable-load escorts and industrial guards they have become part of the everyday scene. The sight of uniformed and helmeted men is no longer one to cause comment; their job is to fit into the normal background, not to attract attention. In some cases, an onlooker seeing a security guard on duty at, say, the entrance to commercial premises could be excused for momentarily mistaking him for a policeman. Indeed the sight of a uniform often instils in members of the public the automatic assumption that the wearer possesses a degree of authority, power and knowledge which is not necessarily true.

What is behind the impressions that are created by the private police of this country? Are they justified or are they without foundation? This chapter will examine the work of today's private detective, and the next, the operations of the modern security company; those areas where the two branches of the industry overlap will also be considered. The scope of those activities is huge and the variety enormous, ranging indeed 'From Adultery . . . To Armoured Cars'.

*

'Private detective', 'enquiry agent' and 'private investigator' are terms which can either be interchangeable, bearing exactly the same meaning, or can be used to connote slightly different elements within the detective profession. It is probably true to say that in general the description 'enquiry agent' is applied to those at the bottom end of the detective industry. In particular it can be used to include the amateur private eye – the postman or bank clerk or shop-owner who makes the occasional enquiry in his locality. Enquiry agent is a term found within the areas of divorce, credit and process-serving work rather than the industrial and criminal fields, and the description 'private detective' or 'investigator' (by which most practitioners prefer to be known) suggests a more professional approach. One of the main reasons why the term 'private investigator' has ousted 'private detective' in popularity is the desire of members of the profession to avoid the accusation of imitating the police in any way. In this book the three expressions are used mainly as interchangeable descriptions of the same individual.

Many people think of the private detective as a solitary figure, a free agent who, on receiving a call from a member of the public requiring his services, accepts or refuses the assignment depending on its nature, how busy he is and how he feels at the time. In fact, although technically he may be his own master, the private investigator is subject to a number of governing influences.

Firstly, the average detective agency employing only a few people relies for 90 per cent of its work on solicitors. The idea of a private detective dealing directly with the public is, for the most part, fallacious. Even those agencies which have ceased to take on matrimonial and process-serving work very rarely look to the individual for work. They may well accept assignments from industrial companies and businesses, but a member of the public would probably be advised to go through a solicitor. In this way, the investigator can 'weed out' the serious caller from the 'crank' and at the same time make the possibility of legal aid available to his client.

Thus it can be seen that most agencies are heavily dependent on solicitors and are therefore anxious to secure the regular 'custom' of as many practices as possible. Similarly, if an investigator succeeds in becoming 'retained' by a company to conduct all its enquiries, this will give a big boost to his business. The private detective's apparent independence is therefore tempered by economic necessity which requires that he provides a satisfactory service and keeps the clients, especially the regular ones, happy.

The influence of solicitors on the investigative profession can also be seen in the way in which detective agencies are now being organized. The 'one-man bands' are still in evidence, particularly among the large numbers of part-time private eyes, but the trend is towards larger agencies modelled on solicitors' offices. Normally there will be one established and experienced private detective in charge and he will employ several investigators to work under him. One development which characterizes the new-style agency is the presence of a back-up force of administrative staff, secretaries and typists who are necessary to deal with the paper-work and report-writing which is now an essential part of a private detective's job. He has to be a good businessman as well as a good investigator in order to be really successful these days.

The amount of money that a successful investigator can earn varies immensely and depends to a great extent on the character of the particular investigator and on the nature of the work he handles. Take the full-time private detective who depends for a living on the success of his agency; he must charge competitive fees, but on a scale which will bring him a reasonable income and hopefully the means to expand. Compare this man with the retired policeman in receipt of a police pension who decides to supplement it by doing a bit of private detective work, or with the amateur private eye who already has a full-time or part-time job, but manages to carry out a few enquiries in his spare time. Neither relies on the money he earns from detection; it simply provides an extra source. Therefore they can afford to charge less, although a wise client will realize that he only 'gets what he pays for'.

The Association of British Investigators has attempted to achieve some uniformity of fees by laying down its own scale which is kept under constant review and which includes suggested rates for investigations, observations, process-serving, court attendances, and expenses such as the use of a car and mileage. For instance, in 1977 the charge for doing investigations and observations during normal working hours was a minimum of £5.00 per hour, rising to £7.50 for the services of a senior investigator; court attendance was charged at £12.00 per half day; and process-serving, within a radius of five miles of the detective's place of business, started at £7.50. These are only recommendations, however, and discrepancies are bound to occur between the fees charged by a large agency operating from business premises and those asked by a private detective using a room in his house as an office, due to the considerable difference in overheads.

In reality the fixed scale of fees is of limited use in ascertaining how much a private investigator can earn because it can be modified by so many factors, the most obvious being that it only applies to members of the ABI. In addition, if the enquiry takes the investigator abroad or necessitates particularly long hours of work or uncomfortable conditions, then the scale will be disregarded and the fees will go up. Similarly, if an agency receives work from abroad then it is entitled to calculate its charges according to the Swiss scale which is almost double the present ABI rate. Then, of course, there are the specialist agencies who can charge more for their services than those who have to compete with hundreds of firms all offering to do the same sort of investigation. The head of one business specializing in commercial, industrial and fraud investigations told me that the fee he charges is regulated by two factors: firstly the length and locality of the job, whether it involves travel abroad or not, and secondly the value of the loss to the client. He estimated that, on average, one assignment would bring in about £2,000, but told me of a recent case involving nine months of investigation for which he received £26,000 (including expenses!).

There is no doubt that there is money to be made in the investigation business. Naturally it is a somewhat speculative profession and depends to a great extent on the economic and legal climate of the day, but most private detectives can make an adequate living out of their profession and a few become very wealthy indeed. It is necessary to add that any private detectives who are prepared to resort to unlawful methods, or indulge in dishonest activities such as industrial espionage, will find that some people are ready to pay a lot of money for their services.

Consideration of some of the dubious aspects of the private detective's work will be postponed until a later chapter. Here it is my purpose only to describe the sort of investigation in which an honest practitioner might find himself involved, although very few investigators would experience every aspect of detective work.

Of the work that comes to private detectives through solicitors, a large amount is process-serving, that is, the service of legal documents such as writs and summonses on parties to legal proceedings. Some private detectives might dispute the validity of including process-serving in a description of an investigator's work, and certainly there is very little detection involved in the delivery of a document to a named address. Nevertheless private detectives are often called in to do this work when the defendant is difficult to find or is deliberately evading service, and for many years now this has come to be regarded as a job for firms describing themselves as enquiry agents and private detectives. Indeed for many agencies this is their 'bread and butter'. This is especially so since the falling off of divorce work, and the demand for process-servers at least does not suffer too badly in times of economic recession because there are the resulting bankruptcies to maintain a steady stream of litigation.

Another common offshoot of the detective agency is bailiff work. Like process-serving this is more a function that happens to be performed by enquiry agents than the true work of an investigator – in Scotland, for example, the same job is undertaken mainly by estate agents – but even so many detectives carry out bailiff work to add stability to their business and thus enable them to get on with the rather more speculative job of private investigation.

On the investigation side of the business, a routine assignment is the tracing enquiry. This may involve locating a missing relative, a beneficiary or a child, or tracing stolen property, credit cards or hire-purchase goods. The private detective may be required to find and interview a witness to a road or industrial accident who has not been forthcoming with his evidence. He may also be employed by a party to civil litigation to find evidence supporting his case – evidence, for instance, as to the nature and whereabouts of a defendant's assets and his means generally, or proof that one party has not been telling the truth under oath in the witness box.

Criminal investigation does not take up as much of the private detective's time as is perhaps suggested by television and other media. Possibly about 10 per cent of his work will be criminal, normally working on behalf of the Defence, checking alibis or looking for witnesses to support the Defence case, but quite often covering the tracks of the police in verifying the Prosecution evidence. Occasionally the help of a reputable private investigator will be enlisted by the police, either officially or unofficially, in their efforts to uncover some criminal activity. I heard of one such case which involved the breaking up of a drugs ring and in this instance the tactic was successful. Furthermore it is frequently the case that during the course of an enquiry evidence of a crime comes to light. The investigator will most likely consult the company or solicitor who is instructing him at this stage and advise that the matter be put into the hands of the police. His evidence will often be needed in the event of a prosecution being brought.

There is a third category of criminal assignments in which the private detective may find himself on the Prosecution rather than the Defence side, and that is in circumstances where a client has not been satisfied with the investigation carried out by the police. Although this is not a very common reason for employing a private detective, it is one which is likely to arise more frequently as the police find it more difficult to keep pace with the increasing number of serious crimes. Even now the police force, especially in London, has been obliged to concentrate most of its manpower into the areas of large-scale theft, robberies and personal attacks. The result is that certain offences involving smaller sums of money have taken a low priority, which generally means that they will not be covered at all. Company losses from internal pilferage or fraud is one area from which the police are retreating, and private detectives are stepping in. The police cannot object to this state of affairs because ultimately a private person has the right to have an investigation made into any crime committed against him. Indeed the police can have no cause to object when, in all probability, if the offenders are found out they will be handed over to them, making a welcome improvement in police detection statistics.

If the criminal side of his work has given the private detective his glamorous image (however misplaced), then there is no doubt at all that it is in the field of the matrimonial enquiry that he has developed his reputation as a sordid 'voyeur' with very few scruples. The situation is a well rehearsed one. Mrs X believes her husband to be committing adultery but concrete evidence must be obtained before the court will dissolve the marriage. So Mrs X engages a private detective to watch her husband. The husband is followed and ultimately (if Mrs X's suspicions are well founded) the private detective will stand up in court and swear that on a certain evening Mr X and Miss Y entered a certain hotel bedroom and that neither left until the following morning. The situation may become more unpleasant if the 'wronged' spouse insists on being in on the 'act of discovery', or, if adultery is taking place in the matrimonial home, the spouse's presence is necessary to enable the detective to enter. On these occasions accusations, recriminations, furnishings and even bullets may start to fly, and at such times the investigator's situation is not always an enviable one.

It must be remembered, however, that in 1969 the Divorce Reform Act changed the law. The old concept of the matrimonial offence, of which adultery was probably the most used, was abolished and replaced by the sole ground for divorce – 'irretrievable breakdown'. The legislation caused consternation in the ranks of private detectives and gloomy forecasts that their livelihood would be threatened. However, mass redundancy among private detectives seems to have been avoided and there are several reasons that could account for this.

There is no doubt that to begin with the demand for matrimonial enquiries dropped off almost completely as people rushed to get divorces under the new provisions, for which purposes the solicitor was now empowered to take the statements himself; but, according to some private detectives, in the last few years the matrimonial market has taken an upturn from their point of view. Adultery still remains as one of the five ways of proving that the marriage has broken down irretrievably as long as it is accompanied by the fact that the petitioner finds it intolerable to live with the respondent, and in addition it is one of only two ways of obtaining a 'quick divorce' without waiting the two-year period needed for desertion or divorce by separation. Therefore, after the first wave of people wanting 'separation divorces' had subsided, there still remained those who had reason for not wishing to wait the necessary two, or in some cases five, years. As well as being a means of proving irretrievable breakdown, evidence of adultery is also being used to some extent to persuade one party of the marriage to give consent to a divorce after two years' separation.

New provisions have now come into force, however, which extend the cases in which parties can obtain 'postal divorces'. This extension will mean the end of the private detective's role (and eventually the solicitor's too) in certain matrimonial areas where spouses are able to apply for a divorce on written forms accompanied by sworn statements. Some investigators believe that this might lead to more approaches to private detectives direct from the public instead of through solicitors, but on the whole it will mean a fall-off of matrimonial work. Their traditional 'adultery-investigation' side will thus be confined to the minority of divorces that are defended and where evidence is still required to be produced in court.

One function in the divorce field that has arisen in recent years, and which will not be disturbed, is the enquiry relating to the financial position of one of the spouses with a view to settling the financial provision after divorce. The husband might want evidence, for example, that his wife is cohabiting with a man who is supporting her, or that she has taken a job which is bringing her £x per week. These are facts which the spouse might conveniently forget when filling in the appropriate form or appearing in court, unless reminded of them.

In the circumstances, divorce work by no means represents the proportion of the private detective's time that it used to occupy. Some smaller agencies relied almost entirely on matrimonial work, but in a recent interview investigator Peter Heims estimated it now took up only 5 per cent of the average detective's business. Therefore it must be assumed that agencies have found enough work in other, newer areas to fill the gap left after the 1969 Law, and that they will find a similar substitute when the work is further decreased by the new provisions.

One of the most important of those new areas, certainly from the point of view of the smaller agencies, which served (temporarily at least) to fill the vacuum, was that of the credit enquiry. The Divorce Reform Act coincided to some extent with an increasing demand from traders, finance houses and businesses for information on the credit-worthiness of customers to whom they were considering selling goods on credit or hire-purchase terms, and private detectives were ready to meet this demand.

Naturally, however, transactions involving credit are not a recent invention. Indeed there are firms and trade protection societies specializing in the investigation and the giving of credit ratings that have been in existence for more than a century. In effect it is an industry in itself, distinct from the private-detective profession, but the beginning of this decade saw a boom in the number of people buying on credit and hire purchase which led to an increased involvement of investigators in credit-enquiry work and the springing up of credit-reference agencies to handle it. Moreover it is relevant to consider this specialized sort of information service here, not only because it provides a source of work for the private detective, but also because it presents analogous problems in the control of its personnel and operations.

In the credit field there is a broad division between credit enquiries relating to businesses and those relating to individuals. The provision of credit references relating to commercial firms is the less controversial side, as the emotive issue of the invasion of personal privacy is not so directly involved. The service offered may consist merely of providing a credit rating against a business for the benefit of a trader who is considering extending credit to that business, or the customer may require a more detailed report containing all the available facts and figures about a particular company. Such a report will probably include among other things a potted history of the company's development and details of its consolidated balance sheet, turnover, pre-tax profit, capitalization and current payments situation. It will give information on whether the firm generally makes prompt or slow payment, and of course details of any history of non-payment.

Some credit-reference firms confine their activities solely to the commercial side of reporting. Dun & Bradstreet of London, part of the giant American-based organization of the same name which constitutes the largest credit-reporting business in the world, is one such firm. It even publishes its own register of businesses which have credit ratings – the 'White Book' of credit. On the other side of the credit business are those agencies which, as well as providing commercial ratings, also deal in supplying credit references on individuals, perhaps the most familiar being the United Association for the Protection of Trade and British Debt Services. This is an area which is regarded with rather more sensitivity by many people, and we shall see in a later chapter that the reason for this is the fact that one mistake on the part of a credit-reference agency can bring untold misery to an individual who gets blacklisted as a result of it.

As with most investigative work, credit information derives mainly from straightforward sources such as public records and journals. On the commercial side, press cuttings, financial columns, trade magazines, Government publications, the Companies' Register, the Register of Business Names and the Register of County Court Judgments are among the common sources. Bankers are also co-operative in those situations where their reference will be of benefit to a client and also, on occasion, when they have been 'bitten' as well and are themselves owed money. As far as individuals are concerned, the most important source of information is again to be found in the

Register of County Court Judgments, and indeed some agencies limit the contents of their files almost exclusively to this readily accessible information.

There are two other important sources of the information that appears on the files of an agency. The first is the subject of the enquiry. Dun & Bradstreet emphasize that in many cases they will go to the firm in question and ask directly about the promptness of their payment and an explanation for any specific complaints from other traders. Unfortunately, particularly in the case of individuals, this approach is not always adopted either because it is impractical or uneconomic, and thus mistakes are made without the subject's knowing about it.

The second important source is that of the actual subscribers to the credit-reporting bureaux. In this respect there is a difference between those agencies which are run for a profit and so-called 'mutual' associations which are non-profit seeking. In the latter cases, subscribers are expected as a condition of their membership to contribute to the running of the association by giving details of any defaulting businesses or individuals with whom they have had dealings. With the commercially run bureaux, on the other hand, there is sometimes no obligation on the subscriber to send information although any such data will be willingly accepted. If, however, a specific enquiry comes up in relation to an individual or trader in a particular district and the agency has no information on them, or has a rather dubious report, then contact is often made with a subscribing trader in that area to see if he has any personal knowledge of the subject of enquiry.

The role of the private detective in the supplying of credit references is two-fold. In the first place, detective agencies now provide an alternative source of credit reporting for traders and finance houses. It is of course true that the great mass of credit business is handled by the large, in some cases computerized, specialist firms. In 1977, for example, Dun & Bradstreet handled about 700,000 enquiries and the United Association for the Protection of Trade estimated that it made about $6\frac{1}{2}$ million searches. Private-detective agencies have provided a more localized service for perhaps a slightly 'down market' clientele.

Secondly, the enquiry agent has in the past performed the function of supplying the larger agencies with information on the credit of named traders or individuals in his locality usually when the agency itself does not have a representative or a subscriber in the district. These agents, known as correspondents, used to be a principal source of information, but they were, and are, investigators of a most amateurish variety, ranging from the milkman or the postman to anyone prepared to conduct a few credit enquiries in his spare time. There has been a steady decline in their use by the large credit concerns for several reasons. In the first place, the inquiry agent very rarely approaches the subject in person; he gathers his information from the rather dubious sources of neighbours, acquaintances and local traders – the 'man in the corner shop' for example – consequently his reports are often inaccurate. Another reason for dispensing with the services of correspondents is their tendency to include in reports gratuitous pieces of information unrelated to credit, concerning the private life and personal morals of the subject. Unfortunately, although reputable reporting bureaux will attempt to exclude such gossip from their files, that is not to say that subscribers are always unreceptive to reading it. Indeed there are those agencies that are not averse to embellishing their reports with some 'juicy titbits' for the benefit of the clients' amusement.

The provisions of the Consumer Credit Act, 1974, which will be looked at in some detail later, have the effect of granting individuals access to files belonging to credit-reference agencies containing information relating to their credit-worthiness. Agencies are therefore tightening up on accuracy and thus use for the old-style correspondent is dying out. In addition, the personal credit boom, which reached a peak in 1973, has seen a reversal as there has been a reduction in the demand for hire purchase and other instalment credit business. The result is that while the larger credit-reference organizations have turned more to commercial reporting and other ancillary services, many of the small-scale agencies have disappeared from the credit scene almost as quickly as they arrived. For some, however, there has been a natural progression from the business of credit reporting to that of debt counselling and collection and in many cases this now constitutes a large part of the work of so-called credit-reporting agencies and of many private-detective firms too.

Debt collection is closely linked with credit reporting, and nearly all the large, as well as the small, firms offer this service. In recent years the law has increasingly moved towards protecting the debtor from harassment for payment and in 1970 the Administration of Justice Act placed limits on the methods that could be used by those seeking to enforce payment of a debt. Debt-collection agencies which confine themselves to legitimate means of collection are therefore more or less restricted to taking over the administrative aspect of collection. Their service now consists of writing letters to the defaulting debtor requiring an explanation for the non-payment. If no explanation is forthcoming, and no money has been received after the third or fourth warning, then the initiative will be handed back to the creditor to start legal proceedings if he thinks it worth the trouble and expense. There are very few threats that collection agencies can now legitimately issue. The advantage of collection being handled by a credit-reference bureau is that there is a warning, either expressed or implied that, in the event of non-payment, the debtor will find himself on the files of the agency as a bad debtor. The collector cannot threaten legal proceedings as he has no right of action, although agencies will often have their own legal department for handling clients' enforcement proceedings. Some debt-collection agencies actually purchase the debts. They will pay the client a sum smaller than that of the bad debt itself and then take over full responsibility for collection. In these circumstances they have all the rights of the original creditor in relation to threatening legal action, but they will be acting unlawfully if the commercial necessity of recovering the purchased debt drives them to resort to more drastic ways of collection. Some of the unscrupulous methods which are sometimes employed will be described later, and it will be seen that it is an area where a measure of justification for the unsavoury reputation of the private detective can be found in the acts of a few individuals.

Up until now this chapter has highlighted those areas of the private detective's work which may give rise to public distaste and mistrust. There can be little doubt that it is the investigator's activities in the matrimonial, credit and debt-collecting fields that are responsible for his unpopularity and for the failure of the authorities to take seriously his claims for recognition and licensing. Private detectives themselves maintain that they are doing a necessary job of work, and that if it is unpleasant at times then the subject of the investigation has only himself to blame for committing adultery or evading payment of debts. Whatever the justifications of this attitude, the fact remains that most people find it hard to understand how anyone can, of choice, make a living out of prying into the lives of others.

For this and other reasons, a few of the larger agencies have ceased to offer these services. King's Investigation Bureau Ltd in London specifies in advertisements that it does not undertake divorce cases or process-serving. Similarly Carratu Ltd, based in Manchester, will only perform such enquiries on the particular request of a regular client. These agencies specialize in the industrial side of investigation, and most firms on an organized scale undertake a number of industrial enquiries of one sort or another.

The employment of private detectives in industry is growing yearly, and there is an increasing tendency for companies, instead of obtaining the services of an enquiry agent through a solicitor, to go directly to a private investigator under the banner of 'security'.

The investigator is increasingly working as an undercover agent at all levels of industry; at managerial and director level to investigate fraud and embezzlement and at shop-floor level to investigate theft and pilferage. Undercover work of the latter sort is an operation of extreme delicacy and may jeopardize the smooth running of the company unless undertaken only with prior consultation and support of any trade union involved. There was one private detective who, in the early days of his business, was engaged to investigate the workers at a factory where a company was losing huge amounts through pilferage. The private detective was not long in finding out who the culprits were, but before steps could be taken the employees found out about the presence of the undercover agent and threatened to go on strike unless he was removed. There was no alternative but to call off the investigation. The private detective in question has never made the same mistake again. He always makes it a condition of any such assignment that the union should be approached and, if the company refuses, he turns down the job. In most cases where consulted, the union representatives or shop-stewards will agree to measures being taken.

At a higher level, a private detective may be called in to investigate the activities of senior employees suspected of fraud or dishonesty and the Younger Committee even reported instances of wives of senior staff coming under the scrutiny of investigators engaged to find out their background, conduct and political leanings.

One of the largest sources of work for the investigator is the insurance company. Naturally insurance companies do not call in private detectives to investigate every dubious claim that comes up; they have their own special investigation departments to undertake this work. But if an enquiry into a claim is bound to be a protracted one, spreading over a period of months, then an outsider is often called in. A common case in which this will happen is the fire-insurance claim where the circumstances suggest that the fire was started deliberately, because then complicated and prolonged enquiries are inevitable.

Possibly the most recent development in the role of the private detective in industry is the importation from America of the idea of pre-employment checks, a procedure which is beginning to take place on a considerable scale. A pre-employment check, which is as commonplace in the United States as the standard provision of references, basically involves the verification of information given by prospective employees on their job-application forms. The obvious purpose of these checks is to weed out unsuitable candidates and in particular to exclude the possibility of a company's employing any applicant with fraudulent intentions. It is also aimed at uncovering fictitious or exaggerated qualifications and at finding out whether the subject has any acute social problems, such as gambling or drinking, which might affect his job performance.

The demand for pre-employment checks is caused to a great extent by the failure of some employers to report to the authorities employees who have committed fraud or embezzlement; they prefer simply to fire them summarily to avoid the bad publicity. It also results from employers' willingness to supply a good reference when dismissing an unsuitable employee in order to save embarrassment.

Pre-employment checks are somewhat controversial in view of the inevitable invasion of the applicant's privacy. In order to be worth while, the check necessitates personal visits to previous employers, interviews with workmates and verification of qualifications. The more senior the post offered, the more thorough the check must be, even to the extent of investigating the subject's personal habits and interests, his marital and social life. This is therefore an area of some sensitivity. The investigator's answer to criticisms of interference with privacy is that a company has a duty to its shareholders to ensure that a prospective employee is suitable and that he is not going to cause the company to lose money through either dishonesty or incompetence.

A further possible development in the vetting of employees, again emanating from the United States, is the use of the lie detector or polygraph. This machine, most commonly working on the principle of analysis of the stress patterns in the voice, has recently been introduced in the UK by a private detective, but its popularity over here has yet to be established. The use of lie detectors raises a far stronger question of the invasion of an individual's right to privacy because they can very easily be used surreptitiously. There are already signs that there would be strong opposition to their use in the interviewing of prospective employees. Recently an officer of the Transport and General Workers Union was reported as saying, 'We would object violently if these machines were used surreptitiously, and I would have thought anyway that this was a general infringement of a person's privacy.' Despite the wide use of lie detectors in America, their acceptability in this country must be severely in question.

Obviously one of the chief reasons for a company's instructing an investigator to conduct a pre-employment check is to discover whether a person applying for a job has any history of dishonesty or criminal activity. Nevertheless, this wish conflicts with another principle of our society, that a man should be given a second chance and not dogged continuously by some indiscretion committed in his past. This principle has been given legal effect in the Rehabilitation of Offenders Act, which was passed in 1974 and came into force on 1 May 1975, and which has caused some concern among investigators.

Section 4(i) of this Act provides that 'a person who has become a rehabilitated person for the purposes of this Act in respect of a conviction shall be treated for all purposes in law as a person who has not committed or been charged with or prosecuted for or convicted of or sentenced for the offence or offences which were the subject of that conviction'; and subsection (2) states that, 'Where a question seeking information with respect to a person's previous convictions, offences, conduct or circumstances is put to him or to any other person otherwise than in proceedings before a judicial authority – (a) *the question shall be treated as not relating to spent convictions* [my italics] or to any circumstances ancillary to spent convictions, and the answer thereto *may* be framed accordingly.' Certain sentences are excluded from rehabilitation, the most important being sentences of imprisonment for life or for more than thirty months. Those sentences not excluded are subject to a rehabilitation period, after the expiry of which the conviction becomes 'spent'. The longest period of rehabilitation is ten years.

If these provisions seem difficult to understand, the effect of them in the context of a pre-employment check is that a private detective asked to investigate a certain applicant should not reveal to his client the fact of any 'spent' conviction relating to that applicant. If, for example, a company director convicted of fraud in 1965 and sentenced to two years' imprisonment applies for a directorship in a client company and the investigator learns of his past conviction, the Act says that he should not advise the prospective employer of the conviction.

Although the provisions of the Act in these circumstances give rise to some concern, the principle of rehabilitation is a sound one and should be observed. Some private detectives are not so convinced, however, and have openly said that in a conflict situation between the interests of the client and observance of the Act, they might consider it their duty to serve the customer first and foremost. Oddly enough the provisions of the Act are, in any case, ambiguous. They only state that the answer to any such question *may* be framed accordingly, and there are no obvious provisions for the enforcement of Section 4, although offences are created in relation to other parts of the Act. It may well be, therefore, that private detectives in the situation outlined above would be acting contrary to the spirit of the Rehabilitation of Offenders Act rather than contrary to the true letter of the law.

It is impossible to consider the private detective's role in industry without linking it automatically with industrial espionage, an activity which will be discussed in some detail later in this book. The Association of British Investigators condemns all forms of industrial spying and reputable firms stress the detective's role in 'counter-espionage'. As companies more and more are beginning to feel the threat of infiltration by both human and electronic spies, so there is an increasing demand for counter-espionage and de-bugging experts, and the ABI has no objection to its members offering these services. The danger is that some private detectives offer their services in this capacity when in reality they are not equipped to deal with the problems. I have been told that there are only a handful of investigators in this country who are capable of uncovering bugging devices successfully, because of the high cost of really effective equipment. Some agencies will offer to do counter-espionage work as a front to their spying activities, and there is at least one known case in which a team of private detectives, called in to de-bug a boardroom, pronounced the 'all clear' and then left their own eavesdropping device.

It can be seen that the range of enquiries undertaken by private detectives is very wide. So far this chapter has described those investigations which make up the normal business of a detective agency, but it would be inaccurate to say that assignments always fall into one of these categories. When I asked Philip Crofts, public relations officer of the ABI, to describe the work of the private investigator, he said simply, 'To investigate,' and this sums it up neatly. A lot of investigative work is, in reality, impossible to classify except in the most general terms such as 'surveillance' or 'tracing' and equally it can be quite unexpected. Most private detectives at some time in their careers receive a request to investigate a case which is out of the ordinary. It might involve flying to the other side of the world, or spending three weeks in continuous surveillance; it will quite probably not fit into any of the types of enquiry discussed above. But so far as the average investigator is concerned, such cases are the exception rather than the rule.

In case the reader is feeling disillusioned at the lack of glamour attaching to the ordinary private detective's lot, I intend at this point to describe the work of one rather special member of the investigative profession. He is the only one I met who in any way lived up to the expectations created by the dozens of television programmes which purport to portray the business of private detection, and do so with monotonous inaccuracy.

Vincent Carratu operates an agency in Greater Manchester which specializes in large-scale fraud investigations and cases involving infringements of trademarks and patents, and the counterfeiting of goods. He is an ex-member of the Company Fraud Squad of Scotland Yard, still retains ties with the police force, and lectures at the Police Crime Prevention College at Stafford. The agency is one of the largest in Europe, and Mr Carratu is 'retained' by a number of multinational companies to handle any enquiries that are needed. He will personally conduct any investigations of particular importance and on some occasions they may lead him into situations of real danger. If this sounds melodramatic, a look at one type of assignment that frequently arises will demonstrate the potential risk attached to his job.

Counterfeit goods are goods which appear on the market bearing the trademark and name of a well-known and reputable manufacturer at a fraction of the normal price. On closer examination it is found that the product is an imitation of the original but of very inferior quality. An example of a product which is quite commonly counterfeited is the long-playing record which comes on to the market in a sleeve identical to that of the bona fide producer, but which has in fact been recorded off the original and is consequently poor in sound quality.

The circulation of counterfeit goods can have a disastrous

effect on the sales and the reputation of a company. It is not enough to trace the distributor; it is necessary to discover the actual source of manufacture of the copies in order to put a stop to the 'racket'. This is where Mr Carratu comes in. He explained to me that the only sure way of finding out the operational base is by infiltrating the gang. It may take weeks of living with them, talking with them, drinking with them before they eventually trust him enough to reveal the factory which is churning out the counterfeit goods. He may have to spend days and nights in a sleazy hotel before the time arrives when the police can be told and the gang 'set up'. Even then the excitement is not over, because when the raid eventually comes, it is usually necessary for Vincent Carratu to be arrested along with his companions to ensure that they do not suspect who informed on them.

This private detective has been involved in dozens of cases of this sort. The products have ranged from perfume to razor blades, and the places he has visited in the line of duty from Belgium to Beirut. Vince Carratu has six sets of identification documents, all in different names, which he uses when he travels abroad to protect his real identity; but he always leaves the country legitimately on his own passport and informs the police in the foreign country of his intentions, because their co-operation is essential for the success of the investigation and his own safety. Mr Carratu told me of one occasion on which this cautious practice of liaising with the police nearly misfired with fatal consequences. It happened when he arrived by plane at Beirut Airport, at the start of an assignment, hoping to arrange a meeting with members of the gang under suspicion. He fully expected that one of their number would be at the airport observing his every move, and was therefore horrified to find that the Beirut police, whom he had informed of his arrival in advance, had sent some men as a 'guard of honour'. Knowing that to leave the plane with them would be to put himself in a position of extreme danger, Mr Carratu could not be prevailed upon to leave until they suggested that he should be handcuffed and led out under apparent protest. When later he managed to meet the criminals, he offered them the explanation that Scotland Yard had warned the Beirut police of the arrival of a criminal fraud expert, and so the police had given him a 'grilling'. They greeted him with a renewed respect.

It must be emphasized that Vincent Carratu is an exceptional sort of investigator who, through his many years at Scotland Yard, is ideally suited to handle this sort of specialist case. Indeed, in many instances he will spend months working on an investigation into a fraud or embezzlement case and at the end will turn over the evidence to his former colleagues who will get the credit for solving the crime.

The majority of private detectives, however, will continue to make a living out of tracing and credit enquiries. It cannot be denied that these are enquiries for which there is a demand from the general public and it is also true that the legal system would be hard-pressed to function without private detectives to serve processes and trace elusive witnesses.

A question that troubles many people is how many agencies are prepared to carry out any enquiry provided the price is right. Great insight into the character of any particular investigator can be gained by asking not only what jobs he would agree to undertake, but also the kind of requests that he would refuse. Private detectives admit that there are members of their profession who will take anything on for a price, be it bugging, telephone-tapping or other dubious activities. There are also those who take advantage of the disturbed people who contact a private detective in the hope that he will rid them of a fear that exists purely within their own minds. Of the investigators that I have interviewed, all said that they would have nothing to do with the 'fairies at the bottom of my garden' caller. Similarly a respectable agency will turn down any job that has a political flavour or any suggestion of strike-breaking about it. Members of the reputable organizations try to maintain ethical standards and refuse dubious enquiries, but it would be contrary to business sense to suggest that they turn down everything which is doubtful. In any event they can all tell stories of private detectives who are in no way fussy about the nature of the jobs they accept.

The private detective's field of work is an ever-changing one. Legislative and economic developments can be seen to have forced investigators to adapt themselves to the needs of their clients, and one-time predominant sources of work have been superseded by areas of new demand. The Divorce Reform Act and recent 'armchair divorce' provisions have compelled private detectives to look elsewhere; many initially turned to the field of credit enquiries and trade-protection services. Now such agencies are doing more debt counselling and collection, while the larger detective firms have looked to industry to provide work in the form of undercover assignments and pre-employment checks.

It was this evolution of the investigator's relationship with industry which led to the latest development in the detective profession: an expansion by some agencies into the field of security services. The trend began with the provision of security consultancy, a service which is now frequently offered by investigators. It was inevitable that, in advising clients how best to secure their goods and premises and reduce shrinkage, private detectives should see the advantage of being able to provide the necessary protection themselves in the form of guard services and alarm systems. A few agencies, either on their own initiative or at the specific request of a client, have therefore started up security sections.

The extent of this development is as yet difficult to judge. Detectives entering this field tend to restrict their services to small-scale provision of static or patrol guards, store detectives and couriers, together with security consultancy.

The interesting aspect of this trend is the fact that it represents a turning full-circle by the private-detective profession which, after all, originated as an offshoot of security organizations at the beginning of the nineteenth century. What is perhaps more important, however, is that it means that the line of definition between detective agencies and security companies is becoming somewhat blurred, making it more difficult to deal with their respective problems in isolation from each other.

3. ... To Armoured Cars

The security industry has three broad divisions, consisting of those companies manufacturing locks and safes (or 'hardware' as it is called in the trade), those producing electronic alarm devices and those providing guarding services. It is impossible to look at one field in total isolation since the science of security is all about finding the most cost-effective combination of those three services in any given set of needs and circumstances; but, as has already been explained, this book is chiefly concerned with the manned side of the security industry and I intend therefore to begin with an outline of the principal kinds of work undertaken by guarding companies.

Having in the last chapter discussed the expansion of the detective agencies into the industrial security field, it is perhaps important to note that there is no comparable movement on the part of security companies into investigative services. On the contrary, there has if anything been a withdrawal from that area. Up until a few years ago Securicor used to run a detective division which specialized mainly in industrial undercover assignments, but it ceased this side of its business after concern had been expressed in several quarters over the propriety of this function. Since that time, the leading security firms have confined their activities in the investigative field to the internal matter of 'vetting' prospective employees. Nevertheless, a number of the smaller security firms continue to offer to conduct investigations, mainly into industrial and counter-espionage matters, as well as providing guarding or other traditional security functions, thus further clouding the definition of the security industry.

There is one area of detection as opposed to prevention, however, which provides guarding companies with a valuable source of work. This is the field of retail-trade security – the provision of store detectives. It is estimated that £500 million plus is lost annually by retailers through 'shrinkage'. The advent of the self-service shop and the modern sales techniques of displaying goods in such a way as to invite the customer to 'help himself' must bear a large part of the responsibility for the bands of shoplifters who provide a headache for the retailer; but shoplifters account for only 25 per cent of the loss. The remaining 75 per cent shrinkage is caused by employee dishonesty and general inefficiency.

The job of the store detective therefore involves directing a watchful eye not only towards the public but also towards the shop staff. There are two ways of attempting to reduce retail losses; the first is by deterring and the second by detecting. If the aim of the shopowner is to deter prospective shoplifters from entering his premises, then the presence of a uniformed security guard or woman 'guardette' will be most effective. If detection of dishonesty is the object, he might hire a plainclothed store detective to mingle with the customers. Very often female employees are trained to do this job as they are less conspicuous among the housewife shoppers. The advantage of the latter course is that the security man or woman working in anonymity can more effectively monitor the behaviour of the staff, without arousing suspicion, by means of test-purchases to check the honesty of cashiers and by spot checks on stock and deliveries.

Retail security staff are also responsible for the stage of security following detection, that is, the arrest and detention of offenders. This is probably the most common situation in which security personnel are required to use their citizen's power of arrest and the difficulties which sometimes face them in this respect will be considered at a later stage.

The leading company in the retail security field is Group 4, which employs 300 men and women especially trained in store detection; but this is an area of overlap between detection and prevention of crime and a local supermarket, for example, might equally well engage a private investigator to do the same job.

Store detection is an expanding source of revenue for security companies and is one of the developments in security brought about by present-day social conditions. However, the two kinds of service traditionally associated with companies such as Securicor are the provision of guards and the secure transport of cash and valuables.

Not so many years ago, the job of guarding industrial premises was left to the gateman during the daytime and the nightwatchman, if anyone, at night. The latter bore a great deal of similarity to the 'Charlies' of a previous century. He was frequently nearing retirement age and unequipped in every way to drive away burglars. Commercial security companies have put guarding on a much more sophisticated footing. The client now has a choice of watch service depending on his needs and financial resources. If the business customer has a large turnover and valuable premises requiring round-the-clock or nightly supervision, then security companies offer 'static guards', that is, guards assigned to one particular site whose job is solely to safeguard those premises. If, on the other hand, the size of the property or value of the contents does not justify the use of permanent internal guards, most security companies will provide a 'radio and beat patrol service' similar to that of the police, except that the guards will be under contract to make a certain number of calls to the customer's property every night. Guard dogs may be used in conjunction with both the static and mobile guards, but the practice of leaving unattended dogs to roam freely around premises at night has been made illegal by the Guard Dogs Act, 1975.

Clearly the static-guard service is the most effective; indeed some security consultants regard the value of mobile patrols as minimal. A well-informed criminal has only to wait until such a patrol completes its round to enter the premises, knowing that the 'coast is clear' for some hours. An enterprise that hires a static guard will almost always make up for the added expense by the criminal loss and wastage saved.

It is erroneous to assume that the only purpose for the presence of a security guard is to scare away or detect the presence of unwanted intruders. In fact this is very far from the truth. The security guard is there to prevent losses of all kind whether by theft, fire or simply wasted electricity. By far the largest part of a security man's time is taken up with closing windows, switching off lights and heating, and locking doors (and even safes) that have been left open.

The greatest losses to industry are caused not by crime but by fire. In 1975 a loss of £212·7 million was attributed to fire damage and its consequences, and is responsible for most of the emergencies that are dealt with by security guards. They work in conjunction with the Fire Brigade and their job is to raise the alarm rather than fight the fire themselves. In the year 1975, Securicor reports that its guards discovered 259 fires in the course of their duties, and in 201 cases the damage was less than £100; in only 21 cases was it over £1,000.

Another area in which the potential value of security officers is now being realized is that of industrial health and safety. Modern legislation imposes a high level of responsibility on employers to see not only that health and safety procedures are laid down but also that they are enforced. Security guards are thus being used to save companies from possible liability under civil law or statute by ensuring that regulations are observed.

Apart from the guarding function of security companies, the other role for which they are well known is that of cash carrying. The armoured-car business, due to its conspicuous appearance, was perhaps the first aspect of commercial security to make an impact on the British public. The sight of uniformed and helmeted men emerging from banks and vaults is now a common one but at first, particularly when batons were carried, it was not so readily accepted.

There was a time when cash and valuables were transported around the City of London in wheelbarrows, but unhappily the days when that was possible have long since passed. It is still quite common for those wishing to transfer cash to send an employee out on foot or by car to do the job, but firms in the business of security regard this as madness. Sooner or later, they say, a criminal is going to become aware of the procedure and an untrained cashier will have no chance of protecting the money and no notion of how to act in the event of an attack.

It may seem to the officious bystander, however, that some security firms have gone rather too far in the other direction. In other words, is it not inviting attack to drive around in a van marked 'Securicor' or 'Security Express' in large letters designed

to catch the eye? Peter Smith, chairman and managing director of Securicor, does not agree. He explained that one of the
reasons behind the conspicuous advertising was that it would
attract more attention and speedier reaction from the public in
the event of an attack than if it were an ordinary unmarked
van. Nevertheless, some companies do not believe in this approach and a vehicle belonging to Brinks-Mat, for example, is
identifiable only by small insignia on its side. Some security
companies in the smaller range provide cash-in-transit services
using plain-clothed personnel and unmarked vehicles. They
state that they believe it to be a safer method of transport, but
others maintain that the real reason lies in the companies' lack
of the capital necessary to set up an armoured-car fleet.

The cash-carrying service offered by many security firms is
one of the most interesting and also most controversial areas of
private security. This is due not only to the fact that it is a
service that brings security companies into the public eye, but
also because in the minds of some people it constitutes an en-
croachment into the public sector. Indeed, before the 1960s, the
safe movement of cash between banks and other businesses was
often achieved with the assistance of police escort, until the
pressure of their other work and an increased demand for police
guards led the Force to abandon this procedure.

Security companies do not deal exclusively in the transport of
valuable goods. Very often the goods are of relatively small
worth, but they are urgently needed in another part of the
country or even abroad. In these cases, when the Post Office
service is considered too slow or too unreliable, there is a
demand for a fast and safe method of alternative transportation; it is this that security companies offer. Consignments for
delivery range from blood plasma and organs for transplant
operations, to computer data or mechanical components for
machinery. Speed, not so much security, is the watchword here.
Securicor have built up a fleet of over 2,000 unarmoured vehicles for this and other non-security purposes.

Another service related to the cash-carrying side of operations is wage packeting and distribution. The client makes out
a cheque payable to the security firm to cover the amount of the
week's payroll and provides details of the sums due to each

employee. The security firm then takes over the whole responsibility of making up the pay packets in the appropriate amounts and will deliver and distribute them on site if necessary. This service therefore relieves customers of the tasks of collecting cash from the bank, dividing it and taking it round to the various 'pay-out' points.

Apart from the major security services, described above, there are many miscellaneous jobs performed by security firms. Most will undertake key-holding for customers, which means they will have possession of a key to the premises in question and will be registered as keyholders with the authorities. If there is an emergency, the police will then call up the security company instead of disturbing the manager or owner of the premises. The provision of security personnel to take normal reception and clerical duties in an organization requiring particularly strict security is another offshoot of the security industry. One of the leading firms has gone so far as to set up a security cleaning division for extremely security-sensitive buildings, and the same company has a section called the 'highway link radio service' which connects commercial drivers with control centres in case of an emergency such as illness, breakdown or even hi-jacking.

The relationship and interplay between the human agent in security and his electronic and fortified allies are not central to the theme of this book, but it is essential to consider this aspect in order to put the role of the security guard into perspective. Peter Hamilton, formerly the honorary secretary of the British Security Industry Association, likened this relationship to an orchestra, in which, he said, 'the instruments of the alarm, the safe and the guard all have to be harmonized'. Each of them fulfils a different function.

In terms of the guarding of industrial and other premises, where the interplay between the three components is at its most pronounced, the object of a security system in relation to unauthorized entry is twofold: to detect the presence of an intruder and to give warning, and to delay his progress for as long as possible. Later it will be shown that similar delaying tactics apply in security transport as well. The basic defence is provided by the structure of the premises itself, namely the construction of doors, windows, locks, etc. The safe or strongroom is the last line of defence and must provide maximum delay. The alarm, on the other hand, must provide warning of intrusion at the earliest possible stage. Alarms may be silent or audible depending on whether the primary object is deterrence or detection of crime, and depending on the function of the particular alarm.

It is not my intention to go into the detailed specifications of the alarms in current use. Suffice it to say that advancing technology means that they are growing in number, variety and sophistication every day. Alarms are not of course confined to the detection and warning of intrusion; equally, if not more important, are those which detect fire and react both to warn of and to extinguish the danger. The cost can range from a few pounds for a single straightforward alarm to thousands of pounds for a comprehensive system to serve the various needs of a large building. Alarms may be set off by sound or movement, using geophones or ultra-sonic rays, and can detect fire by monitoring the slightest rise in temperature. The modifications on a general theme are endless. One large company lists among others, the following detection devices: 'securiwire, frame contacts, magnetic contacts, personal attack buttons, radio bleeps, vibration detectors, acoustic detectors, ultra-sonic detectors.'

There is no doubt that the alarm business is thriving. A large proportion of the many hundreds of security companies are in fact manufacturers of alarms and other warning devices. Alarms are being developed which, in many cases, reduce the necessity for human guards and detectors, or even replace them entirely, thus freeing the manpower to perform other functions.

For many years now the main difficulty confronting manufacturers of alarms has been the high number of false alarm calls, amounting to over 90 per cent of the total calls. Until recently the practice has been to have alarms linked directly to police stations, to enable the police to arrive on the scene as quickly as possible but, understandably, the large proportion of false alarms led the hard-pressed police in some areas to notify occupiers with a very bad record of false calls that they were withdrawing their response to alarms at those premises. This unsatisfactory situation has resulted in police stations refusing to accept direct alarm lines and some companies have been forced to set up their own central terminal stations to take over the function. Direct contact with the police from terminal stations is maintained, however, so the large number of false alarm calls will continue to cause problems for police and security companies alike.

This 'lightning tour' of the security world has attempted to indicate the most important areas in which the presence of private security is to be found today. It is by no means an exhaustive list, but it serves to demonstrate the wide spectrum of the work done by security companies. It can also be seen that not all the services offered are strictly security orientated. In fact they can be divided roughly into those that *save* a business money by protecting it from theft, robbery, burglary or fire, and those that *make* money by increasing the efficiency of the business. Armoured-car transport, store detectives, static guards, mobile patrols, alarm systems, safe and lock devices and fire surveys are all examples of the former, while wage packeting, wage distribution, highway link and speedy delivery services fall into the second category. These 'convenience services' are not the ones which are of concern to the public; it is in relation to 'quasi police work' that security companies sometimes find themselves under public scrutiny, and it is with these aspects that the rest of this book is concerned.

One further development in the story of private security should be mentioned at this stage. This development has taken place within the past few years (although the build-up has been apparent for longer) as a result of the terrorism, both urban and aerial, which has marred the latter half of this century. The effects of terrorism have manifested themselves in several ways. Firstly, it has contributed to the pressure on the police, particularly in the Metropolitan area, which has opened gaps in crime prevention readily filled by private security. Secondly, security consciousness at places of interest, entertainment and business has led to a growth in the demand for guards to conduct bag searches for bombs, and to take the appropriate steps in the event of a 'bomb scare'. Furthermore, we shall see that aerial terrorism has resulted in measures to confer additional powers on certain members of the security industry working the country's airports. Finally, terrorism has led to the establishment of security agencies or new departments specializing in protection against terrorist activities.

The kinds of protection measures which have appeared on the security market as a result of the wave of political bombings and kidnappings that have occurred in the past few years include general advice on how to guard against terrorist attacks, advice and equipment to counter the threat of bombing, and agencies providing executive protection against kidnapping. Most of the well-known security companies have responded to the terrorist situation by supplying products such as 'bomb blankets' together with general advice, but the more demanding work has been left on the whole to specialist firms.

There is one such firm, S & D Security Ltd, which started business in 1974, is run by senior ex-army bomb disposal experts, and offers advice on bomb counter-measures. It found an immediate demand for its services, especially after the Guildford pub bombings in December 1974. Advice on protection against bomb attacks takes the form of surveys of the business in question and the giving of seminars to educate staff and management on the danger of terrorist attack and the precautions that can be taken. This particular firm has also expanded into the manufacturing of equipment especially designed to counter the bomb threat.

Another aspect of anti-terrorist security is that of executive protection. In the *Financial Times* of 11 August 1975, Vincent Carratu reported that, according to the FBI, over 3,500 businessmen were kidnapped in 1974 and that ransom payments varied between $200 and $14 million. Nobody knows how many paid up without telling the authorities. Naturally not all such abductions are carried out by terrorist organizations; in Italy, for example, where kidnapping has grown to the proportions of a national sport, the object is in most cases straightforward criminal gain. But certainly in the UK, or more specifically in Northern Ireland, the abduction of VIPs and industrialists is exclusively politically motivated.

Executive protection again consists mainly in educating the potential victim and those around him to the possible risks. This may involve instruction on house security, on how to check a car for signs of interference or how to drive a car in such a way as to avoid the danger of abduction on the highroad. An employee of the security firm will sometimes spend a period of time with the executive to make sure the lesson goes home. In addition, some firms offer a bodyguard service for persons in positions of extreme vulnerability.

This may all sound rather melodramatic to the mass of the British public. It is hard to imagine many British businessmen hiring bodyguards to protect them. This impression was reinforced to some extent by the head of one executive protection firm which operates in London. He said at a meeting in Brighton in 1976, 'Rich men view with horror the idea of being guarded.' He went on to say that potential kidnap victims did not take seriously the threat to which they were exposed. He gave an example of one rich man who wanted a bodyguard to watch his family while he was away – and do a bit of gardening on the side! It is quite likely that the cost of personal protection is one reason why people shy away from the prospect. It is bound to be expensive because a full-time security presence demands two bodyguards for every client. The normal charge is about £100 per day of eight hours, £300 for round the clock security; and obviously 'part-time' protection is worthless.

Although the use of private bodyguards has not 'caught on' in England, in other parts of the world executive protection is a successful business and, sadly, Northern Ireland is one of the areas which is creating an increasing demand for educational programming against terrorism. The newest development in the Province has been the murder and attempted murder of many leading industrialists, a development which will mean more business to the firms dealing in executive protection.

It must be emphasized that executive protection is a very specialized branch of the industry, and not among the services offered by the traditional companies. On the contrary, a representative of Group 4 expressed the view that VIP protection involving the provision of bodyguards is not rightly within the scope of the private sector and that it is a job that can only properly be performed by the police. It is quite true that it is difficult to see how bodyguards can be expected to act effectively unless they are armed, and obviously they need to be highly trained men.

The question of where the boundary for the activities of private security companies should be drawn is a controversial one. Over the past few years there has been a number of occasions on which public concern has been aroused by the nature of a particular job being performed by a private security company. In 1968 two such instances arose, both involving student sit-ins at colleges. At the Guildford School of Art, the Board of Governors hired security guards, after they had closed the school, purportedly to 'protect equipment'. Athough the authorities explained that they thought the building would be empty, in fact the guards came face to face with the students. Fortunately clashes were averted but the situation caused an enormous amount of concern. In the same year a security company was retained by Haringey Council to evict students 'sitting-in' at Hornsey College of Art. The company in question specialized in the provision of guard dogs and was quite prepared for a showdown with the students. Once again violence was avoided when the students 'came out quietly', but the use of private security organizations to break up student protests was deplored in the press.

In both of the above cases, Securicor had been approached and asked to undertake the assignment but had refused. As the late Keith Erskine said at the time of the Guildford troubles, 'You must not get involved with the public in any way' (Business *Observer*, 6 December 1970). It was Securicor, however, which found itself at the centre of controversy in relation to two other incidents. The first occurred in 1969 when the company was employed to try and prevent gypsies assembling at Epsom during Derby Week. They were unable to do this, but warned the gypsies that their presence was unauthorized and took car registration numbers and names to hand to the police. This would seem to be a clear example of the security company getting too involved with the public in a situation where the possibility of a breach of the peace could not be excluded. Obviously the security guards were operating on private property, but in a situation falling within the *police* function and which could lend justification to the label 'private police' being attached to security companies.

The second security activity concerning Securicor which led to widespread public disquiet was their use by the Home Office to guard persons detained under the Immigration Acts and escort them to detention centres. This practice brought protests from many quarters for the reason that 'While it may be permissible for private companies to show a profit on guarding and transporting the goods of other companies, there can surely be little justification for using such companies as part of the fabric of legitimate law enforcement' (69 *Law Society Gazette*, 673). The National Council for Civil Liberties described it as 'an objectionable extension of power'.

There is no doubt that some security companies continue to cross the line between the private and public area. Recently allegations have again come from the gypsies that in the North there is widespread use of 'private armies' to evict them from sites, and that the methods of eviction employed by these bodies are none too gentle.

The British Security Industry Association lays down limits on the sort of jobs that its members may undertake. The rules state *inter alia* that a security company should not lend itself to the furtherance of any political or quasi-political cause; that member companies should not involve themselves in activities which might be classified as 'strike-breaking', nor in the disciplining or observation of labour in relation to trade-union activities or work efficiency; and that it is not the function of a security company to seek criminals in public places, nor to put down violence in public. Clause (i) of these regulations says that 'no guard company should ever offer a service which might be regarded by the public as a substitute for the use of existing law enforcement agencies, civil or criminal. For example, members would not in general accept employment involving the ejection of trespassers or squatters.' The principle seems clear enough and yet Securicor did involve itself in the eviction of gypsies at Epsom, a job which would seem to fall within this clause; and what of the guarding of immigrants? I asked John Wheeler, director-general of the BSIA. 'Members of the BSIA will not accept any jobs which have political overtones,' he said. 'But is guarding immigrants really a job which has to be done by official security agencies? If private companies can do it more efficiently then it is saving the taxpayer money.' The consequences of undermanning in the police force makes it inevitable that more work, and possibly more controversial work, will be coming the way of private security.

The wide variety of services offered by security companies is responsible for the emergence of a new type of professional adviser – the security consultant. Every single office, factory, bank or other place of business has a unique set of security requirements which depend on the situation, structure and contents of the premises in question. A few firms are in business purely as consultants, but the vast majority offer advice in conjunction with the provision of security equipment or guarding services, or as an offshoot of an investigation bureau. The police themselves have their own Crime Prevention Department which advises on precautions against crime.

One of the advantages of engaging the services of a professional consultant rather than asking for advice from a policeman is that, because the consultant is acting for a fee, he can devote more time to a particular security problem, carry out a survey of the premises, prepare a report and make the appropriate recommendations. This is the sort of detailed study that a Crime Prevention Officer would not have time to go into. In addition, where a situation demands that the client should make use of a security company, the local Crime Prevention Officer can only supply a list of suitable firms in the district; the police are not allowed to show any partiality.

Security consultants, on the other hand, are at liberty to make a specific recommendation of the firm they consider would be the best in the circumstances, but whereas the police are criticized for being too impartial, there is a danger of security consultants suffering from the opposite complaint. It has been suggested that there is a risk of a conflict of interest arising among some firms that offer security consultancy as well as supplying security goods and equipment, either through a desire to push their own brand or because the so-called consultancy firm is in fact 'tied' by way of discount or commission to a certain manufacturer. Dr R. L. Carter, in his pamphlet entitled 'Theft in the Market', concludes that the threat posed by this conflict is relatively small, '. . . because the main buyers are firms which generally know enough to evaluate advice.'

This view was not shared by the managing director of a West London security company who considered that a number of firms describing themselves as security consultants were little more than sales representatives for certain manufacturers of security equipment. He told me of one occasion on which he was asked by an art gallery to recommend a security system in the aftermath of two recent walk-in thefts which had taken place in broad daylight. The owner explained that he had invited two other firms to submit similar advice. The precautions suggested by the company in question consisted of a simple alarm system involving the wiring up of each of the paintings to a central console. The owner of the gallery was impressed by the low cost of such a system, but told the managing director that he was slightly worried because both of the other firms had recommended a sophisticated beam alarm which would operate along the entrance to the gallery. It was not until the security man pointed out that such an alarm would have to be switched off during the day in order to allow visitors to come and go that his suggestion was adopted. He is convinced that the two other so-called security consultants must have been 'tied' to the maker of the beam equipment in a way that clouded their advice to the gallery owner.

I asked Charles Rice, the marketing services manager at Group 4, to comment on this, since his company is one which manufactures its own alarms. He expressed the view, 'In most cases the dangers of partial advice are minimized because the insurance companies, from whom a large proportion of work emanates, will give the client two or three names from which to choose. This means that they can assess the range and price of goods offered and select the most suitable of the suggested companies. Of course, when we advise a customer on alarms, we always recommend one of our own make, but then we have a comprehensive range from which to choose.' Mr Rice went on to agree, however, that there are firms who advertise themselves as alarm companies when they do not make alarms at all; they are simply agents for genuine manufacturers and are accordingly open to influence.

Another explanation for the art gallery story recounted above is that of simple incompetence on the part of the consultants in question. There is certainly no shortage of security services or advice: the problem is one of quality not quantity. It is probably true that a number of people have jumped on the highly successful security bandwagon, not least the private detectives who have expanded into this area. Certainly there are consultants and security operators who do not have adequate knowledge in the field. This is particularly true in the case of companies already in business in a field unconnected with security which, on seeing the potential of the fast growing industry, have started their own security section without possessing the necessary experience; but there is no evidence of widespread incompetence.

On the other hand, according to Dr Carter the main difficulty is that there is also no evidence available on which to evaluate the cost effectiveness of loss prevention. The art of good security consultancy lies in being able to weigh the risk of loss against the cost of security, and in recommending a suitable compromise between the best security precautions available and the price the client can afford. Unfortunately there is no data on which consultants, police, insurance companies or customers can accurately estimate where an ordinary commercial risk stops and where the time for using security services and equipment begins; or can quantify the value of losses prevented by the implementation of proposals or the extent of their deterrent effect.

Despite the fact that economists and clients are somewhat in the dark about the efficacy of industrial security, all the indications are that the demand for loss-prevention services is increasing yearly, and that one of the country's biggest growth industries will continue to expand.

4. Thugs and Bugs

As he spoke, he whipped a tape measure and large round magnifying glass from his pocket. With these two implements he trotted noiselessly about the room, sometimes stopping, occasionally kneeling, and once lying flat upon his face. So engrossed was he with his occupation that he appeared to have forgotten our presence, for he chattered away to himself under his breath the whole time, keeping up a running fire of exclamations, groans, whistles, and little cries suggestive of encouragement and hope. As I watched him I was irresistibly reminded of a pure-blood, well-trained foxhound as it dashes backwards and forwards through the covert, whining in its eagerness until it comes across the last scent.

Thus Sir Arthur Conan Doyle, through the indomitable Watson, described the most famous fictional private detective of all time.

Today, although most investigators would not be averse to possessing the powers of deduction attributed to Sherlock Holmes, they would, I imagine, find themselves at a loss in certain circumstances were they equipped only with a tape measure and a magnifying glass to aid them. Furthermore there would certainly be complaints to the council of the ABI were it known that any of their members were carrying on in such an eccentric fashion!

Technology has made quite remarkable advances this century and security companies have not been slow to take full advantage of it, particularly in the fields of electronic alarms and anti-theft devices and also in the race to produce a more effective armoured car. This chapter is concerned with the methods and equipment employed by the investigator, both on the right and the wrong side of the law, and the influence of technology on him.

As we have seen, much of his work involves routine enquiries and 'foot slogging', serving processes or tracing persons wanted as witnesses or those who have inherited money. In such cases the motive for his investigations is as straightforward as his method in carrying them out. However, by his very nature, a private detective is often employed to carry out a job in secrecy and anonymity. His help is requested to pursue a line of enquiry which the police will not or cannot follow owing to police regulations. Therefore the methods he uses in many cases must be directed towards achieving his purpose while himself remaining 'incognito'.

In the vast majority of assignments, a private detective will carry out an investigation in person, or instruct a subordinate to do so. Occasionally, where conventional methods prove unproductive or impracticable, an unscrupulous enquiry agent may consider enlisting technology's assistance to glean information. Below I shall deal first with the 'manual spy' and his methods, followed by a look at the controversial area of 'bugging' and other electronic devices.

*

As already emphasized, most enquiries are started and concluded without any resort to technical aids. Much of the information which investigators find out on the instructions of a solicitor or client could, they admit themselves, be discovered by anyone with the time, the patience and the inclination. It is a question of knowing where to look among the records, registers, journals and newspapers which are accessible to all members of the public, or who to ring up in relation to a particular enquiry. A credit check, as has been seen, may be carried out by consulting the Register of County Court Judgments, and an industrial enquiry which seems to smack of espionage could well be fulfilled without setting foot on the premises of the company in question, by finding a trade-journal report on the running and affairs of the firm. In these cases, the private detective is being paid for his time and his 'know-how' rather than his powers of investigation.

Many assignments, however, do require that the investigator carries out a period of surveillance on a person or persons. This involves observing and perhaps tailing the subject of the enquiry and is usually conducted surreptitiously. Industrial and matrimonial assignments generally require surveillance in some form – observing the activities of workers in a factory or following the suspected spouse, and this will quite often culminate in direct contact with the subject who may well be encouraged to make a confessional statement if the enquiry needs one.

During the course of surveillance, an investigator might find it necessary to record what he observes for the purpose of proving his case. The use of a camera in these circumstances, that is, photographs taken in a public place where the subject could reasonably expect to be observed, is common and not usually regarded as objectionable. One private detective I spoke to was in the course of investigating a claim for insurance for industrial injury. He had reason to suspect that the claimant, who alleged he had suffered a permanent limp as a result of the accident, was not telling the truth. He had therefore assigned a couple of investigators, equipped with high-powered cameras, to try to obtain confirmation of this suspicion. It is in this sort of case that recorded proof may be essential.

Physical surveillance of this kind, along with the consultation of records and the straightforward questioning of subjects, neighbours, friends, officials and employers make up most of the conventional methods of investigation. A single assignment may take up a tremendous amount of the private detective's time. By illustration, a certain enquiry into the financial means and business activities of a particular man took one investigator down all the following avenues. He started by going to the last known address of the subject and talking to neighbours, local shop owners, the laundryman, the postman and the post office. He then visited members of the man's family, his ex-wife, his accountant, his solicitor and the garage supplier of his Rolls Royce car. The private detective contacted local branches of building societies and insurance companies, and even went abroad to try and find the location of the subject's holiday villa. He consulted local newspapers, the Companies Register, the Electoral Roll, and a credit-reference agency, and when the man was finally located, traced the number of his car, questioned his children and observed his movements over a considerable period of time.

Many of the lines of enquiry in this case proved to be dead-end alleyways, but the investigator achieved the required results in the end. If routine procedures do not 'yield fruit', however, then the private detective may be driven to adopt more drastic methods.

Impersonation is one tactic which he may employ in order to gain information which would otherwise not be disclosed if the identity of the enquirer were known. The impersonation may range from very minor deceptions, such as gleaning information from neighbours on the pretext of being an acquaintance or a friendly insurance man, to the much more serious case of impersonation over the telephone in order to obtain confidential information about a bank account or a criminal record. Most investigators probably indulge in the first sort of deception at some time during their work, but it must be stressed that only the dishonest few resort to the second, more serious variety. The Younger Committee Report lists police officers, social security officials, insurance men, market researchers, telephone engineers, journalists, factory inspectors and prospective employees as among those impersonated.

You would be justified at this stage in asking what the law has to say about this sort of deception, and the answer is that as regards certain impersonations the law is specific and strict. Section 52(1) of the Police Act, 1964, states that 'any person who with intent to deceive, impersonates a member of the police force, or special constable or makes any statement or does any act calculated falsely to suggest that he is such a member or constable shall be guilty of an offence and liable on summary conviction to imprisonment for a term not exceeding six months or a fine not exceeding £100 or to both.' There is a similar provision making it an offence to impersonate officials of the Department of Social Security (now Health and Social Security) under the Ministry of Social Security Act, 1966.

The drawback in prosecuting these offences lies in the nature of the penalties that can be imposed on conviction – a £50 fine has very little deterrent effect on a private detective who undoubtedly charges highly for his unscrupulous approach to the job, and may even add the amount of the fine to his client's bill at the end of the day. Therefore in the past, scope for the court to impose more realistic fines has been achieved by the Prosecution's utilizing the flexible offence of conspiracy which allows for much harsher penalties.

In addition, conspiracy can in some circumstances constitute an offence in its own right, and indeed the crime of conspiracy to effect a public mischief has always proved most useful to the Prosecution in those cases of deception not specifically covered by the two above-mentioned Acts. In 1969 two directors of a company called Tracing Services (Kensington) Ltd were heavily fined for conspiracy to effect a public mischief by allowing staff to pose as doctors, Inland Revenue officials, police officers and Ministry of Pensions representatives in order to trace debtors. Mr Justice Caulfield said in his judgment that a more appropriate name for the company would have been 'Tracing Services (Liars) Unlimited'.

Barrie Quartermain also met his downfall in October 1974 when, amongst other things, he pleaded guilty to conspiracy to effect a public mischief by fraudulently obtaining confidential information from government departments, local government departments, councils and the police. Together with other offences, this conviction resulted in a three-year prison sentence for Quartermain.

Had he been possessed with the power to look into the future, it is very unlikely that Mr Quartermain would have pleaded guilty to this charge, for less than a month later the House of Lords declared that no such offence existed in the case of DPP *v.* Withers. This case involved four private detectives, Ian Withers, his brother Stuart Withers and their respective wives, all of whom were responsible for the running of the London Investigation Bureau. In the course of this business they made enquiries, usually by telephone, to banks, building societies, government departments and local authorities, and to induce the officials or public servants to disclose confidential information they pretended to be acting in an official capacity. They were also found to have obtained information about car licensing numbers from the local licensing offices, and about criminal records from the Criminal Records Office by posing on the telephone as another licensing authority and as the police respectively. This quartet was found guilty of conspiracy to effect a public mischief in the Court of First Instance, a decision which was upheld in the Court of Appeal, but the House of Lords quashed the conviction on the grounds that the offence was one not known to the Law.

It may come as a surprise to learn that the Withers brothers were able to avoid the 'long arm of the law', but in the meantime, Barrie Quartermain decided to appeal against his conviction for a non-existent offence. It is fortunate from the point of view of the public good that, in the case of Withers, the Law lords, among them Viscount Dilhorne, conceded that 'it is possible that if the reference to public mischief had been omitted from counts 1 and 2 the case might have proceeded on the basis that the conspiracy charged in each count was conspiracy to defraud' (conspiracy to defraud being a well-established offence). The Court of Appeal in Quartermain's case was thus able to grasp at this straw, and using its power under the Proviso to Section 2(1) of the Criminal Appeal Act, 1968, upheld that the particulars of the offence disclosed conspiracy to defraud and that the conviction should therefore stand.

The offence of conspiracy is under general review at the moment, however, due to public discontent with its operation in certain fields. Although the crime of conspiracy to defraud was granted a temporary reprieve in the recommendations of the Law Commission, it seems likely that when it comes up for more detailed consideration shortly, it will to some extent be limited in its application, thus losing the flexibility which is the cause of both its unpopularity and its usefulness. As *The Times* of 22 November 1974 said, 'Parliament ... will have to insure that any gaps left by narrowing the scope of conspiracy are filled, if necessary by the creation of new offences.'

One gap has been filled by Section 9(4) of the Rehabilitation of Offenders Act, 1974. This makes it an offence, punishable with a fine of £400 and/or six months imprisonment to obtain specified information from an official record by means of any fraud, dishonesty or bribe. The section is of limited use, however, because it applies solely to criminal records, and then only to those which are the subject of a 'spent' conviction.

The practice of impersonating officials in order to gain confidential information is condemned by the Association of

British Investigators not only because of its unethical nature, but also because quite often there are legitimate means of obtaining the information. Even a straightforward question may sometimes elicit the required answer. For example, one may quite legitimately trace a car registration number to its owner by filling in a form at the local council offices and paying a small fee, provided there is a fairly good reason for wanting the information – that the car was involved in an accident perhaps. Similarly with time and patience a private detective can usually discover whether a certain person has a criminal record of any seriousness by checking up on his previous employment and, if he finds any suspicious gaps when the subject might have been 'out of circulation', by consulting the newspapers at the time for any report of a conviction. The legitimacy of an investigator *passing on* such information to an interested client is questionable, but that it can be obtained without resort to deception is certainly true.

If the law surrounding impersonation by private detectives is in a state of some uncertainty, there can be no doubt at all about the illegal nature of falsifying evidence. This is what one or two of the most unscrupulous investigators have been known to do in order to satisfy their clients' wishes.

In 1972 a headline in the *Guardian* ran 'Divorce Evidence Faked', and continued, 'Scotland Yard has uncovered an "arranged divorce" business which has been operating for at least the last eight years by a firm of private detectives. For fees ranging between £100 and £500, the agency provided "witnesses" and "evidence" for hundreds of clients.' For his fee the client, usually a man, would be provided with a woman who would sign a statement saying that she had had sexual intercourse with the man on a number of occasions. The agency would book the couple into hotels where they would be 'discovered' by private detectives who would make statements to that effect. The wife on finding out about the 'adultery' almost invariably sued for divorce. This contrivance is reminiscent of the old Victorian 'hotel evidence'.

Fabrication of evidence was a method which also found favour with Barrie Quartermain and provided the grounds for three further charges of conspiracy to pervert the course of justice (an offence which, despite the uncertainty over conspiracy generally, is itself bound to remain or be replaced in similar form). In one case he was accused of falsifying evidence in order to procure a divorce for his secretary by persuading her to plant a note on her husband from a supposed mistress and also a pair of red panties in his bed. Quartermain hired two women to 'spike' the husband's drink at a party and take him home where he was conveniently found by the wife's father. The wife was then urged by the private detective to swear a false affidavit and she sued her husband for divorce on the grounds of adultery. The two women involved were described in one newspaper report as 'professional adulteresses' and the Prosecution outlined other cases in which Quartermain had arranged divorce evidence for clients.

An even more disturbing method of obtaining evidence of divorce is that of actually forcing a completely innocent spouse into a compromising position with a girl hired for the purpose, in order to take pictures for use as evidence of adultery. One man was the victim of such a set-up arranged by a London investigation agency. When he failed to respond to the girl's advances as planned, he was physically dragged to bed by three men employed by the agency who then attempted to photograph the couple together. The head of a west-end detective agency was found guilty of conspiracy to pervert the course of justice, given a two-year suspended sentence and fined £2,000.

Another field in which the methods employed may be dubious or even villainous is that of debt collection. As was seen in the last chapter, agencies which carry out credit enquiries are also prepared to do the rather unpleasant job of collecting debts. In addition there are agencies – debt-collection agencies – which specialize solely in this field, and they must be regarded as an offshoot, however indirectly, of the detective industry. The collection of debts is a delicate operation. The law recognizes the need for some pressure to be put on evasive debtors but will not tolerate 'harassment'. The Payne Committee Report on the Enforcement of Judgment Debts gave the following examples of practices of debt-collection agencies which it considered constituted harassment.

1. Frequent calls at the debtor's house, leaving threatening cards.
2. Informing neighbours, local shopkeepers and employees of the indebtedness on the pretext of having another matter to discuss with the person.
3. Threatening to paint over the debtor's car with a statement that it is the property of the creditors.
4. Sending printed notices to the debtor simulating official court summonses, etc.

The Younger Committee Report also mentioned the practice of sending a van marked 'Bad Debt Collection' to wait outside the debtor's house, and Donald Madgewick and Tony Smythe in their book *The Invasion of Privacy* describe a case in which a debt collector picked up a child from school, telling the headmaster that the mother was in hospital. In fact he wanted to obtain the parents' new address from the child.

In 1970 a law was enacted in an attempt to curb the activities of these 'strong-arm' collection agencies. Section 40 of the Administration of Justice Act provides that:

A person commits an offence if with the object of coercing another person to pay money claimed from the other as a debt due under a contract he:

(a) Harasses the other with demands for payment which in respect of their frequency or the manner or occasion of making any such demand or of any threat of publicity by which any demand is accompanied, are calculated to subject him or the members of his family to alarm, distress or humiliation.

(b) Falsely represents in relation to the money claimed that criminal proceedings lie for failure to pay.

(c) Falsely represents himself to be authorized in some official capacity to claim or enforce payment, or

(d) Utters a document falsely represented by him to have some official character or purporting to have some official character which he knows it has not.

The Act appears adequately to protect the interests of debtors and stop harassment from collectors, but the National Council for Civil Liberties is concerned about how the Act will be interpreted by the courts and what they will consider constitutes 'harassment'. Patricia Hewitt, general secretary of the NCCL, explained, 'We have not yet heard of a successful prosecution under the Act, therefore we are not in a position to say whether it has gone far enough towards protecting debtors.' I have found evidence of only one such prosecution, reported in the *Investigator* of April 1973, in which a married couple trading as the Trade and Professional Credit Register were fined £50 for harassing a debtor, but as they pleaded guilty to the charge and the nature of the harassment was not described, it is impossible yet to judge if the Act will be a sufficient protection against this abuse.

The 'strong-arm' tactics that have been described in relation to some private detectives' methods are, it must be emphasized, practised by only a few members of the profession, and the same must be said of the use of surreptitious surveillance devices, described in the next section of this chapter.

*

In 1970, during the debate in the House of Commons on the Right of Privacy Bill, its sponsor, Brian Walden, MP, made the following statement: 'There is no doubt about what is happening in terms of "bugging". The use of bugging devices and the planting of microphones has now become common practice among private detectives and enquiry agents.' This allegation was hotly, and it seems probably rightly, disputed by the Association of British Investigators. Nevertheless it is a problem which is on the increase and one which merits careful consideration. Therefore before discussing the incidence of bugging in this country, it is first necessary to define what is meant by the term 'surreptitious surveillance devices' and to describe some of the forms in which these devices are currently to be found.

The expression 'technical surveillance device' could include anything from a motor car used for tailing a subject to a highly sophisticated miniature microphone, but those with which this chapter is concerned are aids which provide an 'electronic or optical extension of the human senses', the human senses in this case being sight, hearing and memory. Furthermore, those devices used solely as an aid to memory, such as the camera or tape-recorder, cannot be regarded as surreptitious when utilized normally to record what the investigator or other user sees or hears in person. It is for this reason that the camera was considered as an extension of the 'manual spy' rather than as relevant to this section. The Younger Committee on Privacy decided that a technical surveillance device becomes objectionable when, 'were it not for the use of the device, that person [the object of surveillance] would be justified in believing that he had protected himself or his possessions from surveillance whether by hearing or observation.' It is equipment falling into this category that I intend to discuss here.

As far as devices for visual surveillance are concerned, they can be divided into those used for viewing and those for recording. In the first category, there are telescopes which are so powerful that they make it possible to observe places where the occupant could reasonably be expected to be protected from the public eye. There are also miniature lenses which can be placed in a hole drilled in the wall and allow the 'planter' to observe what goes on in the room. 'One-way windows', which appear solid from one side but which act like a window from the other, can be employed in surreptitious visual surveillance. Another aid to observation and 'tailing' is a variety of fluorescent powders and dyes which, if applied to the subject being followed (either secretly put on his clothing or added to aftershave or hair lotion), are invisible except to an investigator focusing an infra-violet light-beam on the subject.

In the field of visual recording, cameras have been so miniaturized that they can be concealed in rooms or on the person, and devices developed to enable pictures to be taken on a given occurrence (for example, on a person entering a room) or simply at regular intervals. There are now methods, using for example infra-red light or light intensifiers, enabling pictures to be taken in the dark or while the photographer is moving.

Furthermore, by means of a telescopic lens, recordings can be made of otherwise secret activities or objects. Some years ago, while Lord Denning was engaged in examining the security implications of the Profumo affair, the *Sunday Times* published a picture of him at work at his desk. The journalist reporting the story disclosed the contents of a confidential letter lying on the desk at the time, which had been made legible by the use of a telescopic lens, in order to highlight the vulnerability of public figures and top-secret information to surveillance and spying. The situation is made more dangerous by the advent of optical 'scanners' which can, it is said, scan and record all kinds of documentation at a rate of 840 single-spaced typewritten pages per hour.

Perhaps the most incredible device of all, however, is an aerial hovering device described by Alan F. Westin in his work *Privacy and Freedom* as

a unit with two counter-rotating blades which is sent to hover aloft attached by a cable to ground control equipment. About three to four feet in diameter and weighing 40 to 50 pounds the surveillance unit now carries close circuit TV equipment that transmits pictures of objects at ranges of a mile or more. It could carry listening equipment just as easily. The unit hovers at an altitude of 100 to 2,000 feet and rotates 360 degrees for tracking purposes . . .

The implications of such a device would be far-reaching.

In terms of auditory surveillance, the most publicized devices are the 'bug' and the telephone 'tap'. The 'bug', which has attained notoriety through frequent intrusions into the lives of screen spies such as James Bond, is technically a microphone using a radio link – that is to say it needs no wires because the built-in radio transmitter is battery operated. It is said that a one- to two-ounce battery allows for continual transmission for four and a half to five days. Advanced technology means that microphones can be manufactured which are no larger than a match-head. They can be concealed in anything from a sugar cube to a pair of cufflinks, and easily planted in a boardroom or under a bed. There are even firms abroad which specialize in producing furniture, fittings, office equipment and ornaments, all with built-in microphones.

These 'bugs', despite their minute size, might be detected by an experienced private investigator conducting a room search, but there are others which do not need to be planted inside the premises. Directional or 'parabolic' microphones, for example, can listen in on a conversation within a building from outside. Some of this variety require an open window or door in order to function, others can pick up sounds from an entirely enclosed room, although their range is more limited. In the open air directional microphones can tune in on conversations hundreds of feet away.

Similarly the contact microphone, which is attached to the outside of the wall of a room, is undiscoverable except with the use of electronic equipment. It operates by picking up and recording the sound waves that hit the wall and these can be transformed back into words. An addition to the contact microphone, the 'spike mike', is for use when the walls are too thick. The spikes, which are placed in the wall like nails, transmit the vibrations to the contact microphone which records them.

More bizarre variations of the 'bug' include 'micro-balles' which, it is reported, can be shot from a special rifle and embedded in the wall near a window to transmit conversations from within; and also the radio pill, a miniature transmitter for tailing which may be swallowed by a person without his knowledge. It has even been said that a dentist can insert a microphone into a tooth cavity during the process of filling it and that the device would be capable of transmitting everything said by the victim for the period of a day.

However all these 'bugs', although difficult and sometimes impossible to discover by the physical searching of premises, are susceptible to detection by electronic equipment which has been developed as a counter-measure. This equipment is often nothing more than an AM/FM transistor radio receiver which becomes an effective anti-bugging tool by scanning the frequencies on which room bugs most commonly transmit. If there is a device transmitting on a frequency that is scanned, there will be a 'feedback' reaction, that is a high-pitched sound on the detector, which will inform the operator that the premises are bugged.

A microphone may also be connected by a wire link, either specially laid or using an existing pair of wires. In this case there will be no 'feedback' because no radio signal will be emitted, but the chances of physical detection are increased because this method normally requires some sort of recording machinery, unless the eavesdropper has access, for example, to the next-door room where he can listen indefinitely. Usually, however, the microphone will be wired to a tape recorder, and although

these can now be obtained in sizes no larger than a cigarette
packet, the drawback with a tape is that, like the battery of a
'bug', its life is limited. This problem can in part be overcome
by using a mechanism that induces the tape recorder to self-
activate on hearing a sound and stop when silence returns; but
this is not altogether reliable as the machine may be activated
by a vacuum cleaner or decorators in the room before picking
up anything of use to its owner. The fact that a tape recorder
would have to be collected is a further hazard. Nevertheless it is
a less expensive method than the radio 'bug' and although in-
stallation and collection may create difficulties, on some occasions whole buildings or suites may be wired up with great
ease during construction.

The other main abuse covered by the Younger Committee
definition of surreptitious surveillance is telephone 'tapping', an
activity which is highlighted from time to time in Parliament
and elsewhere, though quite often in reference to state rather
than private interference. There is more than one way to tap a
telephone. The traditional tapping of a telephone is done by
physically intercepting the GPO line at any point before it
mixes with other wires at the central exchange, and this can be
done fairly easily at terminal boxes inside the building. The
common tap of this sort uses the telephone current for power
and, because it approximately halves the voltage passing
through the victim's telephone, is easily detectable by a counter-
bugging investigator. The likelihood of detection can, however,
be reduced by using either a separate source of power for the
amplifier or a 'parallel tap' powered by a battery. The disadvantage of the latter is that it necessitates regular replacement
of the battery. Most of these devices can utilize recorders which
may operate from the time the receiver is lifted to the time it is
replaced in order to conserve power or tape.

Eavesdropping on telephone calls can also be achieved without cutting or breaking into GPO wires by the use of an 'induction coil'. This device must be placed within four feet of the
telephone and works by utilizing the magnetic field of the telephone itself to pick up the sound pulses and transmit them to a
receiver. Finally, the simple substitution of a bugged microphone in place of that of the GPO in the mouthpiece of the

telephone is an effective way of intercepting calls. These last two methods should more accurately be classified as 'bugging'. Since both involve the use of radio-linked mircrophones, both are discoverable by electronic means.

Apart from microphones and telephone taps, other devices for auditory surveillance include 'trail bugs' (the radio pill is only one of a number of varieties) which have a range from a few feet to several miles, and 'laser microphones' which, providing there is nothing to impede the line of sight, can send out invisible light beams over a distance of miles. When these return from the target, they are in a modulated form which can be transformed into sound.

There are many precautions that can be taken to minimize the chance of having confidential conversations overheard. These vary from the de-bugging equipment described earlier, to scrambling devices for telephones and 'window oscillators' which break up voice patterns and thus prevent surveillance from outside. However there are two devices in current use which are more alarming and potentially dangerous than all the rest because of the difficulties in detecting them.

The first is known as the 'infinity transmitter' and is technically a tone-activated hookswitch by-pass which works along the following lines. The device is wired into the telephone of the prospective victim and then, when the private detective wishes to start eavesdropping, he dials the number and by pretending to have got the wrong number induces the victim to replace the receiver. The line is still open, however, and by sounding a predetermined tone the eavesdropper activates the infinity transmitter which has the effect of enabling him to listen in to anything that is said within earshot of the telephone, whether the receiver is on or off the 'hook'. In England the device can be defeated by making sure that any 'wrong number' caller hangs up before replacing the receiver, the drawback being that few people ever suspect that they are being bugged. In America, where the telephone system is different, a similar device can be activated by dialling the last digit of the telephone in which the device is installed. Thereafter it records anything that is said within earshot of the telephone and the bell is prevented from ringing. As to detection, the infinity transmitter can be discovered by a 'tone sweep' through the possible range of activating sounds, but already bugging experts are introducing modifications, such as a two-tone activator or a prolonged-tone activator to counter the detection equipment that is on the market. The fact that, theoretically at least, this device can be activated from any part of the world poses an enormous threat to privacy and security, meriting particular attention.

The second piece of equipment was described to me by a private detective who had seen it demonstrated in Brussels. He said of it, 'It was built into the electrical wall socket and therefore a visual search would fail to reveal it. It was fed by the electric circuit and therefore did not need its batteries changing and would live for ever. It could be turned on and off by remote radio signal and consequently if it was turned off while a sweep was being made could remain undiscovered.' How, then, can businessmen engaged in top-secret discussions be absolutely sure that they have not got an uninvited listener? The same private investigator had this to say: 'I make the suggestion that they hire an aeroplane and hold their conference above the clouds.'

The natural follow-up to any discussion of technical surveillance devices is the question of how much bugging actually goes on in this country. It is well known that the use of such devices has presented a major problem in the United States, but is it right in this instance to assume that 'what happened in American yesterday, happens in Britain today'?

To try and ascertain the numbers of surveillance devices used is obviously a difficult task. In 1972 a BBC programme, 'The Burke Special', which reported on infinity transmitters stated that there were only four such devices in this country, a number which, even allowing for a substantial increase since then, does not seem to present much cause for concern; but considering the damage which could be done to the profits of a commercial company or the reputation of an individual by their use, even four infinity transmitters are four too many. Furthermore, the maker of the 'electric-socket bug' claimed this year to have sold a number of these devices in Britain. It must be presumed that much of the equipment sold in this country is in the hands of people describing themselves as private detectives, but it is probably those who offer counter-espionage services as a guise to their real activities as industrial spies, rather than ordinary investigators, who make use of this sophisticated equipment.

Ordinary radio-link microphone 'bugs' would be more within the reach of the average private detective, but my own researches on the subject have necessitated the conclusion that Brian Walden's allegation of widespread use overstated the situation. There are naturally difficulties attached to estimating the amount of bugging, which by its very nature is surreptitious and intended not to be discovered. Nevertheless, many members of the investigative profession think that the issue of bugging has been exaggerated. One private detective told me that in his whole career he had only ever discovered three bugs, and another investigator with great experience in the industrial field said, 'This "bugging" thing has been blown up out of all proportion. In the twelve years that I have been running my agency I have only discovered three bugging devices, one of which was so amateurish as to be laughable. It consisted of a microphone concealed in a book which had the middle removed and was left on a boardroom table.' The Younger Committee on Privacy, who closely examined the use of technical surveillance devices, also concluded that they figured 'in only a small percentage of private-detective work'.

There is, however, one device which does feature more significantly than the others and that is the telephone tap. The reason for this is that when done with the subscriber's consent, telephone tapping is not a criminal offence. This method has therefore been particularly effective in matrimonial enquiries where the husband or wife has consented to the telephone being tapped. The Association of British Investigators has always condemned this practice as being unethical, and this is still its official view despite the fact that ex-president George Devlin had this to say on the subject some years ago:

The writer has on a number of occasions over the past few years obtained evidence by means of tapping a telephone, and on no occasion has there been any adverse comment or criticism by any Judge, Magistrate, Barrister or Solicitor, save the defence on pleas on behalf of the guilty party concerned that 'it is not cricket' to tap telephones. This has been dismissed, the view being that it is 'not cricket' to commit adultery ... I tend to tap a telephone as a last resort when all conventional methods of detection have failed for one reason or another.

It seems fair to assume that if members (however few) of a respectable association admit to having tapped telephones, then less reputable private detectives would have little compunction in resorting to these methods; and it appears that the less scrupulous are even prepared to utilize the illegal method of 'tapping' by using a bugging device in the mouthpiece. A manufacturer of these devices is reported to have sold about 10,000 of them in this country. Mr Peter Heims, a former president of the ABI and one of the leading protagonists in the 'clean up of the private detective's image' campaign, has spoken out strongly against the use of all kinds of technical surveillance devices. However, even though he insists that well-respected professional investigators do not (and indeed have no need to) resort to electronic aids and emphasizes that the Association is firmly against their use, he was, in 1973, forced to admit that, 'There are unscrupulous private investigators operating in England who will install bugs at very high fees to which they add the amount of their fine should they be caught ... There are a number of firms who openly advertise this type of equipment for sale which shows that there is a demand, and if there is a demand, there must be a use.'

The law has failed to keep up with the advances in technology which have produced the sophisticated bugging equipment now on the market. One ex-commander of the Metropolitan Police to whom I spoke expressed the view that bugging devices in this country are less easily obtainable than in other European countries, but if this is true it must be as a result of good fortune rather than good regulation. Private detectives themselves say that, on the contrary, they are not difficult to get hold of, and may cost as little as £12. They are certainly openly advertised in several magazines which one can find displayed on any bookstand. In an August 1976 edition of *Exchange and Mart* there were no less than four different varieties of 'bug' offered for sale; some of the advertisements included the fact that the device was not licensable in the United Kingdom while others omitted to mention it. The devices were described variously as a 'Super-bug', a 'professional miniature F.M. wireless microphone . . . much smaller than an ordinary matchbox' and a 'James Bond type bugging device'.

The Wireless and Telegraphy Acts of 1949 and 1967 provide more or less the only legislation in this area. Section 1 of the 1949 Act makes it an offence to install or use any apparatus for wireless telegraphy except under licence from the Ministry of Post and Telecommunications. 'Wireless telegraphy' is defined in such a way as to exclude any device using wires. Section 5(6)(i) of the same Act prohibits the use of wireless telegraphy apparatus with intent to obtain information as to the contents, sender or address of any message, and subsection (ii) makes it an offence to disclose information so obtained. This provision might appear ideally suited to discourage the bugging variety of telephone taps, but since the maximum fine after one offence is still only £50, any vestige of a deterrent is swept away. The penalties for contravention of Section 1 are likewise totally inadequate, ranging between £10 and £100 and/or three months' imprisonment depending on the nature of the apparatus.

Section 7 of the 1967 Wireless and Telegraphy Act gives the Minister of Post and Telecommunications power to make regulations forbidding the manufacture and importation of wireless telegraphy equipment for the purpose of preventing or reducing the risk of interference with wireless telegraphy. One such Order is in force applying to radio telephonic apparatus operating within certain frequencies common to bugging equipment, but the import restrictions are being evaded by manufacturers who send devices in 'kit' form, containing the necessary parts and instructions on how to assemble them.

Ultimately the disadvantage of all these provisions is that they were not intended to counteract bugging. As the Younger Committee said, '[Their] purpose . . . is to safeguard the radio wavelengths from unauthorized interference rather than to protect privacy.'

As far as telephone tapping is concerned, the law is even more inadequate. A private investigator who fits a device to intercept calls may commit the civil tort of trespass to property against the Ministry of Post and Telecommunications if he interferes with the external telegraph or telephone wires, or against the householder if the interception takes place on the internal wires. If, however, he obtains the consent of the subscriber (or possibly his wife) to tap the line, he would not even commit a civil wrong. The only offence that he might commit if he used a device which ran off the current, would be that of dishonestly causing electricity to be wasted or diverted, contrary to Section 13 of the Theft Act, 1968. Once again though, this Act was intended to deal with the theft of much larger quantities of electricity than would be used in this instance.

Incredible though it may seem, the above measures constitute all the legislation that exists to control the unauthorized tapping of telephones and the use of bugging equipment by private detectives or other private individuals. More substantial penalties can again be imposed by utilizing the offence of conspiracy. Conspiracy to contravene the Wireless and Telegraphy Acts was the third charge that Barrie Quartermain found himself facing in October 1974, and he heard counsel describe the 'Watergate armoury' of bugging devices and electronic equipment that had been discovered in his network of private-detective agencies. The presence of the conspiracy charge helped to enable the Court to send him to prison for three years, but the recommendation of the Law Commission is that the maximum penalty on a charge of conspiracy to commit a summary offence (an offence under the Wireless and Telegraphy Acts is only triable summarily) should be one year's imprisonment, and although the fine would remain unlimited, this is hardly a sufficient deterrent to the unscrupulous investigator.*

We have already seen how the decision of the House of Lords in the Withers case swept away the offence of conspiracy to effect a public mischief. One result of this decision is that there will be no repetition of the conviction recorded against a private detective named Graham Blackburn in 1974. Mr Black-

---

* In fact Parliament has imposed considerably more limitations on the scope of the offence of conspiracy and on the penalties available for its commission than were recommended by the Law Commission. See Part I of the Criminal Law Act 1977, which came into force on 1 December 1977. The Act has the effect of leaving us even less well-protected against certain patently undesirable invasions of privacy than we were before it was passed.

burn, an ex-detective of the Leeds police force, pleaded guilty to 'effecting a public mischief by tampering with Post Office equipment and intercepting, tape-recording and listening to telephone calls made by or to the occupant of a house in ... Leeds' (*The Times*, 6 June 1974). The Law lords in DPP *v.* Withers declared that there was no substantive offence of effecting a public mischief. The Law Commission admitted that the decision left an unfilled hole in the law as far as cases such as that of Blackburn were concerned, but they considered those cases to be rare. The judge who ordered Blackburn to pay a fine of £500 on his conviction took a more robust view of the situation when he said, 'Whatever the legal technicalities, this offence constituted a very serious invasion of privacy.'

Later in this book, there will be an examination of the ways in which other countries have sought to regulate such activities as well as the proposals that have been voiced in England to deal with the problem. There have indeed been many determined calls for legislation. In July 1975, staff of the *New Scientist* went as far as planting a 'bug' in the House of Commons which transmitted Members' conversations to a receiver on Westminster Bridge, in an effort to impress on the Government the potential dangers of the situation. To date, however, those calls for reform have been ignored in legislative terms and the law remains impotent to deal with a worsening threat to privacy.

5. A Farewell to Arms

Members of the police force have, as we know, authority granted to them by Common Law and Statute to carry weapons, make arrests and conduct searches in certain circumstances and under certain conditions. As already mentioned, it is not unknown for a member of the public to mistake private detectives or guards for regular policemen, and in particular a blue uniform or an identity card (probably only intimating membership of a private-detective association) may very easily mislead a person into thinking that the bearer possesses all or some of the above powers, or at least that he has a right to insist on co-operation.

In June 1973 Mr Clinton Davis asked the Secretary of State, Sir Geoffrey Howe, that powers of search, detention or arrest without warrant, and of the exercise of force beyond Common Law and existing statutory powers conferred on persons, other than constables, were currently available to employees of private security companies or firms. The answer from the Secretary of State was, 'None ... beyond those of any other private citizen' (House of Commons Reports, Vol. 858, Paragraphs 237–8). In other words, the security guard (or private detective) has no more powers than you or I. It is therefore necessary to discover what those powers are in order to see how they can best be used by security companies to run an effective service and how far employees can protect themselves or their clients' property from criminal attack, within the confines of the law.

As far as powers of search, detention and arrest are concerned, the law is complex and difficult. To lay hands on another against his will and without lawful excuse is an assault. Unlawful detention, including arrest, is false imprisonment. Both are crimes and civil wrongs. The question that arises is in what circumstances the detention and arrest of suspected criminals is justified by law.

Even the police have no general power to arrest and detain a person on a criminal charge. They must normally have a warrant which must comply with certain specifications. However, under some circumstances both a police constable and a private citizen may arrest someone without a warrant, though the conditions of arrest are more stringent for the latter. A constable may arrest without warrant anyone whom he reasonably suspects to have committed an arrestable offence, even though no such offence has in fact been committed (as long as his grounds for believing an offence to have been committed are reasonable). The private citizen on the other hand, may only make a lawful arrest of '(a) one who is for whom he reasonably suspects to be in the act of committing an arrestable offence, or (b) one who is or whom he reasonably suspects to be guilty of an arrestable offence, where such an arrestable offence has been committed' (De Smith, *Constitutional and Administrative Law*).

The difference between the powers of the constable and those of the private citizen is, therefore, that in order for the latter to make a lawful arrest on suspicion of guilt, an arrestable offence must actually have been committed – no defence of reasonable belief in its having taken place exists.

Security guards occupy this more risky position along with all other private citizens, and thus store detectives and similar guards have to think carefully before they arrest or detain a suspect, because they may well find themselves liable for an offence or a civil wrong. If, for example, a store detective were to arrest a shopper outside the premises with an article which was not paid for and that shopper later convinced a court that she simply forgot to pay, then the store detective would be technically liable for wrongful imprisonment. It is a subject on which all security personnel should be made aware of their rights and limitations.

As to search, under normal circumstances, a citizen has no power to search another, but it is possible for individuals to agree to being searched. Such a clause is often written into employees' contracts to enable security men at, say, factory gates to make spot checks for pilfering; or it may be made a condition of entry into premises that a search should be conducted, a practice which has become common in the aftermath of the terrorist bombings in this country.

This then is the position in law in relation to powers of search, arrest and detention that applies to you and me. It therefore follows that it should apply to employees of security firms similarly; and it does, with one significant exception. In 1973, in the face of frequent hi-jacking of aeroplanes and terrorist activities centred around airports, the Protection of Aircraft Act was passed by Parliament.

The Act provides in Section 10 that:

(1) For purposes to which this part of the Act applies, the Secretary of State may give a direction in writing to the manager of any aerodrome in the United Kingdom requiring him to use his best endeavours to secure that such searches to which this section applies as are specified in the direction are carried out by constables or by *other persons of a description specified in the direction* [my italics throughout].

(2) The searches to which this section applies, in relation to an aerodrome, are searches:

(a) of the aerodrome or any part of it.

(b) of any aircraft which at the time when the direction is given or at any subsequent time is in any part of the aerodrome, and

(c) *of persons or property (other than aircraft) which may at any such time be in any part of the aerodrome.*

Section 11(2) of the Act provides that the Secretary of State may make a direction to an operator of an aircraft or the manager of an aerodrome specifying measures which may include the provision of persons charged with the duty '(a) of guarding the aircraft, or (b) of guarding the aerodrome, or persons or property (including aircraft) in any part of the aerodrome, against acts of violence'.

The powers given in the above two sections are further augmented by the provisions of Section 19(2) which says that:

Without prejudice to the preceding subsection, where a direction given under Section 10 of this Act to the manager of an aerodrome is for the time being in force, then if a constable, *or any other person specified in that direction* in accordance with that section, has reasonable cause to suspect that an article to which Section 16 of this Act applies [that is broadly a firearm or explosive, or imitation of such, or any other weapon] is in, or may be brought into, any part of the aerodrome, *he may*, by virtue of this subsection and *without a warrant, search any part of the aerodrome or any aircraft, vehicle, goods or other movable property of any description which, or any person who, is for the time being in any part of the aerodrome, and for that purpose:*

(a) may enter any building or works in the aerodrome, or enter upon any land in the aerodrome, *if need be by force,* and

(b) *may stop any such aircraft, vehicle, goods, property or person and detain it or him for as long as may be necessary for that purpose.*

This is an extensive quotation from the Act, but necessary in view of its importance in the context of this book.

It is quite apparent that, at the time of the passing of the Act, the chief class of persons that it was contemplated would be covered by a direction under Section 10, was private security personnel employed either by the Airports authority, or under contract. Obviously the police, under whose jurisdiction the airports now fall, could not be expected to be responsible for all the policing needed in them, especially for conducting the baggage and personal searches that have become necessary. It is therefore unavoidable, if unfortunate, that this task should be entrusted to civilians, and private security employees are an obvious choice.

It is of course true that for several years private security guards have been used to conduct the searches at embarkation points. This they are empowered to do by virtue of the airlines' ability to make such a search a condition of boarding an aeroplane. The 1973 Act goes further by giving the persons specified in a direction under Section 10 the power to search anyone on the aerodrome and to detain them if necessary.

In fact, as yet no direction has been made under the Protection of Aircraft Act. The airlines continue to conduct searches on the same basis as before and security guards are not yet authorized to use more powers than any other citizen. The airlines have been willing to co-operate with, and follow advice given by, the Department of Trade, because not only can they now be compelled to take such steps under the Act, but the

Department has the additional sanction of being able to withdraw the grants it now gives to airlines to help pay for security. Nevertheless the searchers and guards at embarkation points are in a position of great responsibility and some danger. As yet there has been no call for these security guards to deal with armed terrorists, but how they would react in such a situation is a question of some concern.

In circumstances in which a direction has been given, there is scope within the Act to deal with the very real danger which might be caused by the employment of guards without adequate training or experience. Section 12 enables the Secretary of State to specify the qualifications of the person authoritized in the direction, and 'qualifications' include training and experience.

In fact, although no directions have been made, there is already some form of training among airport security men. There are training courses run by the Department of Trade and the individual airlines. The Chief of Security for British Airways explained, 'we insist that before a private security man works for us on screening duties he goes through either the Board of Trade course or the British Airways programme. They are trained how to spot a terrorist or hi-jacker, how to react in the event of trouble and how to co-ordinate with the police who are always in the airport. We spot-check the men sent to us by private security companies to ensure that they have attended one of the courses.'

This sort of precautionary training is obviously essential in view of the delicate job of these guards. Some airlines are not as careful as British Airways, although the general standard at British airports is high.

Although the Protection of Aircraft Act has not yet been invoked, it is the first step towards the extension of powers of private security guards as against other private citizens, and anxiety and anger were expressed by police and public alike at the time of the passing of the Act.

In a letter to the Home Secretary published in the *Observer* on 2 September 1973, Inspector Reg Gale complained that the police had not been consulted about the Bill (as it then was). In the letter he said:

When one takes personnel such as these who are not vetted, selected or trained to the standards of a constable and who do not hold office of constable and places them in a situation where by law they have the right to detain and search members of the public, it must give cause for concern. Further when this searching can produce a situation that has occurred recently at a foreign airport where terrorists armed with automatic weapons and grenades will use those weapons when discovery is imminent, then the training of these security personnel can only be regarded as completely inadequate to deal with the situation.

The Protection of Aircraft Act does provoke some thought about the future direction of the security industry, and some problems. It is obviously essential that standards of training should be maintained, because here is a situation where private police, in very nearly the true sense of the words, are operating in the place of regular policemen who have years of training behind them, while private security guards do not even have the benefit of a criminal record check against their names.

Some policemen see the Act as just the beginning of an extension of the powers of security companies and their personnel. The authorities insist that, in all other respects, security-firm employees are treated as any other private citizen. In practice, however, whatever their legal rights and powers, *de facto* security personnel are often treated differently from other individuals. A small instance can be seen every day of the year in the shape of the armoured cars that can be found parked on double yellow lines outside banks, supermarkets and the like. Naturally no one begrudges security companies their aim to reduce 'pavement time' to a minimum, but in fact their legal liabilities are often waived by the authorities. Another serious example lies in the batons which security men were allowed to carry for so many years.

Reg Gale fears that the Protection of Aircraft Act may be the thin end of the wedge that will eventually lead to security firms being allowed to arm their men, but the 1973 Act specifically prohibits this in Section 13 and the possibility of this ever happening seems a long, long way away. Nevertheless the issue of arming is a live and emotive one requiring examination and discussion.

The past few years have seen an increase in the number of policemen carrying firearms while on duty. This fact was highlighted not so long ago when a bank robber was shot dead by a plain-clothes policeman who happened to be passing the bank on his way to another assignment when the crime was committed. Nevertheless the policeman on normal patrol has never carried a gun as part of his uniform, and this situation seems likely to remain in the future. In nearly every other country in the world the civil police are armed at all times. Furthermore, in the United States of America it is regarded by most people as their constitutional right to possess arms in order to protect their property, and in many states permits are easily obtained to enable a citizen to carry a concealed weapon with him to protect his person.

In England it is of course also possible for an individual to obtain a firearms certificate entitling him to own a gun. Indeed, up until the end of the 1950s it was quite common for these certificates to be granted to security couriers and guards. One man who has been in the security business since 1946 said that to begin with he always used to carry a gun whenever he was in charge of valuable goods, although he never had to use it. However, by the beginning of the 1960s the attitude of the police was changing and they had begun to cease granting firearms certificates to persons employed in security, and to encourage those who already had guns to surrender them. Opposition to the practice of security men carrying guns came to a peak early in the decade when the attention of the public was drawn to it by an incident in which a privately employed security guard shot and 'winged' an attacker. From that time increasing pressure was put on certificate holders, and the arrival on the security scene of the large, organized security company saw the departure of the gun and its replacement by the baton or nightstick as a means of protection.

For many years the sight of the security guard openly equipped with such a weapon was an accepted one, criticized only occasionally by members of the police force and public – that is, until the year 1973.

Section 1 of the Prevention of Crime Act, 1953, provides that, 'Any person who, without lawful authority or reasonable excuse, the proof whereof shall lie on him, has with him in any public place any offensive weapon shall be guilty of an offence.' In 1973, three security guards were convicted under the Act. The guards were members of a security firm called Wight Star Securities which was described as reputable. At the time of the incident which led to the prosecution, the guards were employed at a dance hall. Each carried a truncheon which according to the defendants acted 'as a deterrent' and was 'part of their uniform'. They appealed against conviction on the ground that they had 'reasonable excuse', a question, they argued, which should have been left to the jury to decide. The Court of Appeal, although accepting that it was for the jury to decide on the question of reasonable excuse, nevertheless upheld the conviction, probably because the judges felt there was no possible evidence on which the jury could reasonably have found for the defendants. In passing judgment, it was stressed that 'weapons must not be carried as a matter of routine or as part of a uniform'. It is by no means certain that the law prohibits the carrying of batons in *all* circumstances. The Appeal Court indicated that guards might be justified in carrying weapons if they were in immediate danger of attack; if, for example, there had been a series of attacks on security guards, or they had information which led them reasonably to believe that such an attack would take place. The test appears to be 'imminence' as opposed to 'expectation' of attack, which limits the defence to a narrow category of circumstances and means that, as a general rule, the courts will not tolerate the carrying of truncheons.

Since that decision, and despite the derisory fines imposed on the defendants (reduced by the Court of Appeal to £5 each), security companies have abandoned the practice of arming their men with batons. Most appear to have resigned themselves to this interpretation of the law and indeed the majority were quick to say that they considered truncheons unnecessary anyway. The British Security Industry Association has pronounced itself fully opposed to the carrying of such weapons and now supports a policy of 'no batons' along with that of 'no guns'; but the transition to the present state of affairs was not without protest. It was at one time reported that one of the biggest of Britain's private security forces had been asking the

Home Office for permission to arm its guards with nerve gas guns; and that the main private police forces were chafing under restrictions allowing their men to carry only small sticks. Most firms, however, have now come to accept the position.

Nevertheless small pockets of resistance to the disarmament of security companies still remain. There is one firm based in London that believes it has a case for the controlled arming of its men. Brinks-Mat, although it is not one of the biggest guarding companies, has a significant place in the security industry. It specializes in the transportation of bullion and high-value loads which may run into millions of pounds. In the field in which it operates, the company does not consider that it has any real competitors; it numbers the Bank of England among its regular clients. Because of the huge amounts carried, Brinks-Mat feels there are special circumstances which govern its desire to arm its men. To begin with, the company differs from other security companies in that it expects its employees to make every effort to protect the property entrusted to their care, even to the extent of risking life if necessary. By contrast, Group 4 and Securicor, for example, rely on a policy of delaying assailants; but once delaying tactics are exhausted their men are instructed to hand over the valuables and co-operate entirely with the criminals. The justification for this policy can be well illustrated by the case of an attack on a security guard which occurred on 11 November 1976. The guard, employed by Securicor, was collecting money from a bank when he was held up by four raiders who told him to hand over the £4,000 that he was carrying. Instead of doing so, the guard put the money into a chute in the van which took it out of the reach of the attackers. Their answer was to shoot him at point-blank range with a shotgun. At the time of writing, the victim is still critically ill in hospital. There can be no doubt of the courage of this security guard, but he might have avoided injury had he followed company regulations.

Very few people would expect a man to risk his life to protect another person's property. Brinks-Mat do expect their men to make every effort to defeat an attack, although they have no criticism of guards who do hand over the goods in the face of an armed raid; but then Brinks-Mat have experienced only a handful of attacks in the fifty years of their operations despite the nature of the loads they carry, and no fatalities. What worries Peter Cox, the vice managing director, is the ease with which criminals can now successfully attack cash-carrying companies. The armed criminal is at an enormous advantage over the security guard. In 1975, there were 391 robberies in which firearms were used. In 1976, the percentage increase in the reported use of firearms generally was greater than the percentage increase in any of the main groups of indictable offences, rising 49 per cent, and the reported use of shotguns in robberies rose by 62 per cent. There is no doubt that a large number of these robberies took place on security firms and that most were successful.

There is one obvious consequence of these statistics which is very disturbing: the fact that large amounts of cash are regularly finding their way into the criminal underworld. Some will probably be used to develop more sophisticated methods of attacking security firms; and one thing is certain, while the odds remain in favour of the robber, the number of attacks is bound to increase.

There is strong evidence from Europe, where most guard companies are allowed to arm their men, that arming would discourage attacks. The difference on the Continent, however, is that the regular police, too, are armed. In this country, as Peter Smith, chairman of Securicor, explained, 'While our policemen remain unarmed, the public would never stand for security guards being allowed to carry guns.' On balance, the public is probably right. The reduction in robberies and attacks on security companies that would be achieved, however desirable, is outweighed by the disadvantages and dangers of allowing bodies that are in no way accountable to Parliament or the public to arm their men. It is impossible to conceive of a state of affairs which would allow persons who are under no official control, who are not required to undergo any sort of training, who may even have criminal records, to carry truncheons or batons, let alone firearms. This view, I believe, will always prevail against those who are in favour of arming, and puts the arming of security guards quite out of the question.

There are of course ways other than resorting to arms in which security firms can make the odds in favour of the criminal less attractive, but private security is a commercial enterprise and running through the whole industry is the basic exercise of balancing risk against cost. This purely economic consideration of cost effectiveness means that in any given situation, the possible security measures available have to be compromised to satisfy the two interlocking requirements of acceptable risk and acceptable price.

A good example of these principles at work can be seen in relation to the armoured vehicles which are a well-known feature of many security companies. The extent of the protection offered by the so-called 'armour' depends on the type of job for which the vehicle is being used. Naturally even the strongest armoured cars are not designed to resist *any* form of attack, and indeed in Canada a raid on a bullet-proof vehicle was successfully carried out using an anti-tank weapon. This is the kind of eventuality that cannot be provided for but, in addition, only a very small proportion of security vehicles are armoured in the sense of being bullet-proof. To be really bullet-proof, both the bodywork and the glass of the security vehicle should be impenetrable by a bullet fired from any normal gun at close or long range. It is only a few bullion carriers that can claim to be armoured in this way and the reason is one of simple economics. If a security company is carrying cash or valuables worth millions rather than thousands of pounds, then the client will be prepared to pay more for the service and the security firm can offer more costly security precautions and equipment. If, on the other hand, the vehicle is being used to make collections or deliveries of relatively small amounts – the morning's takings, the week's wages – then the cost of acquiring a completely armoured car would outweigh the risk involved and the economics of security would be upset.

A compromise is therefore necessary, and with regard to security vehicles the compromise takes the form of different standards in the quality of the protective shell of the vehicle. Next in strength to the bullet-proof armoured cars are those that are fitted with a bullet-resistant body and windscreen, designed to withstand bullets fired from a distance but susceptible to penetration at close range. By far the most common form of security vehicle, however, is the light-armoured variety. This consists of an ordinary commercial vehicle strengthened on the inside of the bodywork and side windows by a steel mesh which, although not secure against the most powerful firearms, offers protection against most guns if fired from a distance. The windscreen is usually of toughened glass and will stand up to a certain amount of battering; it is not, however, bullet-proof or bullet-resistant. Most of the security vans seen on the roads are light-armoured, and most of the cash carried by security companies is carried in these vehicles.

As can be seen, therefore, the term 'armoured car' is for the most part a misnomer. Very few attacks occur on security vehicles themselves, so that commercially the risk does not justify the expense of using bullet-proof materials. Occasionally, however, something happens to upset the normal risk factors. There was such an occurrence on 28 March 1976, when a Securicor vehicle was attacked on the A2 and a security employee shot dead by the robbers. In this case the criminals forced the van to stop and then managed to batter in the toughened windscreen. They made one of the guards open the back of the vehicle and escaped with most of the load. The windscreen should not have given in under those circumstances and since that time Securicor have expended both time and money on finding out what went wrong and with putting it right.

It is a natural reaction in this situation to take the view that a little more thinking and testing before the event, rather than after, might have saved a life, but in Securicor's defence it must be said that this was the first attack of its kind: in 99·9 per cent of cases a raid will take place while the load is being carried either to or from the security vehicle. However it does provide an example of how a necessary commercial decision (in this case to use a light-armoured vehicle for cash-carrying) can have graver consequences in security than in any other industry.

It is also true to say that in some instances a lack of foresight is a criticism that *can* justifiably be levelled at members of the security industry. One of the ways in which security companies can make life more difficult for the would-be robber is by using their intimate knowledge of the patterns of this very specialized crime. For instance they know, as we have seen, that the vast

majority of attacks take place 'on the pavement'. They also
know that the assailant likes to have his getaway car as near as
possible to the scene of the crime. Yet it was left to an outsider
to suggest to one of the leading companies that by using a
specially designed trolley, too large to go into an ordinary car,
for carrying the goods across the pavement, they could greatly
hinder attackers, who would be forced to use a more conspicuous van or truck as a getaway vehicle. To its credit the
company in question immediately produced a prototype trolley
for experimental purposes. In the event it proved to be awk-
ward and unwieldy and the guards disliked using it, and so the
project was abandoned.

Perhaps surprisingly, the moral of this story to my mind is
not that suggestions which might prove to be expensive mistakes should be ignored, but rather that there is room for *more*
research within the industry. After all, it is impossible to be able
to gauge the effectiveness of any particular measure without
trying it out, but it *is* important that the industry itself should be
producing the ideas for improvement. There is, of course, a
great deal of research done by the industry, and some of the
leading companies co-operate in their findings in an effort to
achieve the best possible results. This is important because in
my view the security industry owes a higher responsibility to the
public than many other industries, since it is striving to prevent
the losses of cash which, although they represent only a small
proportion of the total amounts carried, are nevertheless
significant. The question is whether some security companies
could spend less money on advertising the effectiveness of their
security and rather more on improving it.

Another facet of this responsibility arises in relation to the
problem of balancing the profit motive against the need to
maintain certain standards of practice. There is an enormous
number of security companies competing in the security field.
This can lead to a security price war, with some firms trying to
undercut their rivals, and even adopting commercial tactics
such as 'loss leaders' to attract custom. This is not a widespread
practice and many companies refuse to cut their charges and
compromise their standards, relying on the customer to appreciate that 'you only get what you pay for'.

This leads conveniently into an aspect of security which is emphasized by members of the industry, namely the fact that a not inconsiderable part of the responsibility lies with the clients themselves, and this view is reinforced by the increasing number of robberies taking place actually on the premises just *after* a security company has delivered its load rather than during delivery.

It is the view of some security experts that the security industry in general is underpriced. They say that people are reluctant to pay for security, that they buy security because their insurance company tells them to, but that they shop around for the cheapest rather than the best. Thus the client often bears part of the blame for faulty alarm systems or poor guarding services.

In addition, the client's co-operation and help can, in many cases, materially reduce the risk of loss and this is particularly true in the field of security transport. The risks of transporting cash and valuables can be reduced to a minimum if the security vehicle can drive into a secure, enclosed bay for loading and unloading. Most of the large financial institutions which require the carriage of large sums of money and bullion have special security loading areas built into their premises, thus cutting out completely the high-risk 'pavement time'; so the educating of builders, architects and clients to the necessity of incorporating basic structural security facilities is important.

Even this is not a foolproof procedure unless the staff and management of premises can be impressed with the necessity of observing security measures as much as the security guards themselves. This was shown all too clearly in March 1977, when a Brinks-Mat armoured car drove into a loading bay at Heathrow Airport. Once the doors were safely closed behind them, the security men handed over the consignment which consisted, among other things, of diamonds. Unfortunately the building was not as secure as had been thought and armed robbers had managed to get into the premises before the van arrived through another entrance. They got away with £825,000, but this was a lesson to the Heathrow authorities rather than to the particular security company.

In any event, it is apparent to anyone working in the big cities that, in most cases, security firms are not afforded the luxury of drive-in facilities. Their vehicles can be seen parked on the kerb outside banks, shops and offices. In these circumstances firms rely heavily on regulations and discipline to ensure the safety of their men and their clients' property; regulations such as restrictions on the amount of cash to be carried at any one time, or compulsory radio check-ins to a central control station at frequent intervals. What may appear to be petty rules are in fact vital to security in a situation where guards are so vulnerable to attack.

So far, this chapter has been chiefly concerned with the cash-in-transit side of the security business. Naturally internal and patrol guards can also be targets for attack. For many years, one of their most useful 'weapons' against assault has been the guard dog.

The dog is, of course, a recognized agent in both crime prevention and detection, used widely in the police force for functions ranging from stopping escaping criminals to sniffing out heroin or explosives. It is not surprising, therefore, that the dog found a place in the private security industry also, but unfortunately a lack of control in this area meant that some security companies misused a weapon that is potentially as dangerous as any gun. Instead of using dogs only in conjunction with handlers, as in the police force, security firms hired out dogs as custodians in their own right, particularly for those customers who could not afford the expense of paying for an internal guard or for a visit by a mobile patrol. In other words, the security company would deliver one or two Alsatian dogs to the client's premises in the evening, and simply release them into the building or the compound surrounding the property to roam uncontrolled. The dogs were often neither trained nor suitable; they were frequently badly treated and under-fed and their instinct to attack was obviously encouraged. The result was inevitable. There was a series of tragic incidents, nearly all involving children, in which untethered guard dogs made savage attacks. In several cases the victim was partially to blame. He had perhaps climbed over a wall or through a hole in a fence, and may have been trespassing, but this was not important. What was important was that a number of children were killed or severely injured by vicious dogs left to roam in otherwise empty premises.

As a result of public disquiet, many of the well-known companies ceased the practice of hiring out unaccompanied guard dogs, but some other firms continued to use dogs in a thoroughly irresponsible manner. On 15 July 1968 the *Sunday Times* ran an article on the Hornsey Art College troubles when Haringey Council hired a security company to stop students getting in and out of the college. Securicor turned down the contract because of its political implications but they supplied a list of those firms that might agree to do the job and at the top of the list was A1 Security Dogs. The head of the company made no bones about the way he would have liked to deal with the students if the Council had given him the backing. 'I would have charged into the college like a bull at 2 a.m. in the morning and set the dogs among them. I could have cleared the place in an hour.' Alternatively he suggested: 'The Council should build an eight foot wire fence around the perimeter. Then they should leave a pathway about ten feet wide and build another fence. I could put my men and dogs in the no-man's-land. We would put the place under siege. If the students tried to get in or out, my dogs would rip them to pieces.' Of his dogs, he had this to say, 'Securicor people say that my dogs are uncontrollable and vicious beasts. This is not strictly true. My dogs are friendly until they receive commands; then they're killers.'

This sort of attitude naturally led to calls for control over the use of guard dogs, especially in circumstances when they were allowed to roam loose. For many years demands for action went unanswered, until 1975 when the Guard Dogs Act was passed by Parliament. The Act provides that:

A person shall not use or permit the use of a guard dog at any premises unless a person ('the handler') who is capable of controlling the dog is present on the premises and the dog is under the control of the handler at all times while it is being used except while it is secured so that it is not at liberty to go freely about the premises.

In addition a person who keeps a dog at 'guard-dog kennels', that is, at a place where a person in the course of business keeps a dog which is used as a guard dog elsewhere, is required under the Act to hold a licence issued by the local authority. The local authority may impose conditions, and the licence may be cancelled if the holder is convicted of an offence under the Act, or certain other offences relating to the treatment of animals.

The use of guard dogs by security firms has declined since the passing of the Act; they are no longer such an economical method of security. In addition, the value of the guard dog as a protector (as opposed to a detector) has been called into question in recent years. The argument is that while a man and a dog may represent one and a half good guards, if the dog is injured by an assailant, the human element of the partnership loses some of his value because of anxiety for the dog. Therefore the man and dog team has declined in popularity as well as the use of the dog on its own. Unfortunately it cannot be said that the passing of the Act has wiped out the latter practice altogether. Instances of guard dogs being left without handlers can still be found; after all, the kind of people who are prepared to leave savage dogs unattended are not above a little law-breaking if necessary. Other security firms have been more resourceful. *The Times* of 31 January 1976 reported in the wake of the Guard Dogs Act, 'Some firms have recruited geese as substitute custodians for vacant premises at night.' An American security company found a more macabre solution by enlisting the help of a tarantula spider in the guarding of a jeweller's window. Personally, I hope that this is one idea which is not copied in this country.

The Guard Dogs Act is certainly a welcome and much-needed piece of legislation, controlling an area of the security industry that has seen some abuse and too many unfortunate accidents. It also serves to show that, on a small scale at least, licensing to control certain aspects of security can be introduced, although it is yet to be seen how well it will work.

The use of the guard dog, now subject to the restrictions imposed in the legislation, is the last remaining 'weapon' available to the security officer in his attempts to protect his client's property and his own safety at the same time. On the public highways, the security employee is without even his dog. Security companies must now look for ways of making their loads less attractive to criminals by decreasing their chances of success. This 'lengthening of the odds' can only be done by means of careful planning, strict discipline, intelligent thinking and, in some cases, more expenditure on research, instead of by means of the gun, the truncheon or the nightstick, because it is quite clear that on the whole the security industry has, for better or worse, bid a 'farewell to arms'.

6. A Cause for Concern

There is a rotten apple in every barrel, so they say. The age-old maxim records a sad truth that attends all walks of life. The cause for concern is that a rotten apple in the barrel of security can have far more serious consequences than in most other fields. In their respective professions, both the private detective and the security officer have access to potentially damaging information, be it in relation to a person's character or his credit-worthiness, or to a company's premises and its movement of valuables. This is a situation that is full of temptation and open to abuse.

Not unnaturally, it is the bad elements of the industry that so often attract the most publicity. In a court case in January 1970, in which a private detective was sentenced to four years imprisonment for perjury in a matrimonial matter, Judge Edward Sutcliffe said: '. . . the divorce courts have to rely on the complete integrity of the enquiry agent. It is only because enquiry agents, as a whole, observe these rules of integrity that the courts can work at all.'

An example of integrity apparently deserting another investigator is provided by a case which was reported in March 1976. This enterprising private eye, in an effort to generate work for his struggling business, took a trailer tent from a camping shop, and then returned to offer his own services to recover it – for 10 per cent of the article's value. In fact his only reward was a conviction for attempting to obtain money by deception.

Possibly the only encouraging aspect of this case is that such unethical behaviour (even although it does not constitute a bar to practising as a private detective) does at least fall within the scope of the criminal law. As has already been shown this is not always the case, particularly with regard to the gaps left un-plugged by the disappearance of the offence of conspiracy to effect a public mischief and a private detective does not necessarily break the law even if he causes distress and embarrassment to an individual by behaviour that is patently undesirable. Equally an investigator can cause distress and embarrassment without any dishonest intention on his part, simply by careless-ness in the handling of the confidential information to which he has access. This can be well illustrated in the field of credit en-quiries. The various sources of the information provided by credit-reference agencies and by some private detectives have already been described. Some are clearly questionable: there must be strong doubts about the reliability of information gained from part-time enquiry agents and casual checks with local traders as to the credit-worthiness of individuals or firms, and this is now recognized by many organizations. But mistakes also occur with some regularity in relation to the procuring of information from public records or subscribing firms.

A very understandable reaction in this situation is to observe that if a firm publishes a credit report that is untrue, then it must surely be guilty of libel. The law, however, is anomalous in this respect. For the purpose of libel actions, it draws a dis-tinction between profit-seeking and non-profit-seeking trade-protection associations. In the case of London Associations *v.* Greenlands, 1916, it was decided that reports on the credit of individuals made by non-profit-making groups for the pro-tection of their trade were covered by the doctrine of qualified privilege – meaning that in order to sustain an action in libel, malice on the part of the writer must be established. It is prob-able that, by analogy, communications to such an association by members reporting on others are also privileged. The obvious danger of this situation is that sometimes less care is taken to avoid inaccuracies than would be the case if the threat of a libel suit existed.

Profit-making organizations have no such protection under the law against the consequences of publishing libellous matter about an individual. They have to be careful, therefore, about the accuracy of the information going into a report, but most admit that by guarded comments and other indications it is often possible to convey the gist of an uncorroborated piece of evidence detrimental to the subject.

The value of libel proceedings is further reduced by the fact that where a bad credit reference is given as a result of a mistake, the victim may never find out why he or she is being refused credit. An error leading to a thoroughly credit-worthy person being placed on a blacklist may come about in several ways.

A simple case of mistaken identity can cause undeserved hardship to an individual. If a Mr John Smith disappears from an address in, say, Preston and a different John Smith moves into a house in the same road, the bad debts of the original Mr Smith may be attributed to the newcomer. Mr K P was the victim of a similar error. He was refused credit on several occasions although he had no idea of the reason. Eventually he found he had been blacklisted for alleged County Court judgment debts spreading over a period of four years. In fact these debts had been incurred by his father who had been ill for some time. The NCCL contacted the United Association for the Protection of Trade who agreed to rectify the mistake.

A straightforward clerical error can cause similar distress to a completely innocent person. Another common instance of unjustified blacklisting occurs when a bill for payment is disputed by one of the parties on the ground that the goods supplied are not satisfactory. Mr A disputed a bill from his garage and, for some time, refused to pay. Eventually he did so, but the damage had been done; he was already on a blacklist despite the perfectly reasonable explanation he had for withholding payment.

It is quite common for credit-reporting bureaux to list debtors by address as well as by name, but it has also been known for such a bureau to list *only* by reference to address, the object being to overcome the problem of debtors who change their names in order to avoid being traced. The danger is that a person moving into a house previously occupied by a bad debtor may find himself refused credit simply on the basis that he resides at that address.

The anxiety and humiliation which a person must feel when

he is refused credit for no apparent reason can turn into a nightmare if he finds himself being harassed into paying a debt about which he knows nothing. In 1972 Mrs A received a letter informing her that the debt she had run up on her Personal Shopping Card at a certain store had been handed over to a firm of debt collectors. In fact, Mrs A had never used her own Personal Shopping Card and furthermore the number of the Card which had incurred the alleged debt was different from her own. The ruthless methods employed by some firms of debt collectors are unpleasant enough for those who genuinely do owe money; if the 'victim' is innocent of the charge, the methods must become doubly distressing.

The situation obviously could not be allowed to continue in which an individual, finding himself unjustly blacklisted and refused credit, had no recourse. As early as 1971 Leslie Huckfield, MP, said, 'Perhaps the major factor separating credit investigations from other private detective work is the right of the individual to know what's going on.' Eventually, in the face of enormous pressure to legislate – pressure from Leslie Huckfield in the form of two Private Member's Bills and from two Government Committees (Younger and Crowther), the Consumer Credit Act was passed containing provisions to deal with the licensing and control of credit and hire business *and* of ancillary credit businesses, which include credit-reference agencies.

The Act defines a credit-reference agency as 'a person carrying on a business comprising the furnishing of persons with information relevant to the financial standing of individuals, being information collected by the agency for this purpose', and 'individual' includes a partnership or other unincorporated body but not a company. It requires that such an agency must obtain a licence from the Director General of Fair Trading, and the licence, which may be a standard or group licence, will only be granted if the applicant satisfies the Director that, among other things, he is a fit person to engage in the activities covered by the licence.

The Director is instructed to have regard in particular to whether the applicant has ever been convicted of certain criminal offences, or offences under the Consumer Credit Act, and is entitled at any time to refuse, renew, vary, suspend or revoke the licence.

The most important provisions from the point of view of the private detective involved in credit reporting are those contained in Sections 157–60 of the Act. These provisions give the debtor or hirer the right to know the name of any credit-reference agency to which a creditor, owner, or negotiator has applied for information about him, and a right for a small fee to request the agency in question to show him any file it holds on him. If the consumer considers any entry in the file to be incorrect, he can ask for it to be removed or amended. If the agency refuses to do so, the consumer may ask the Director for an order which, if executed, carries criminal sanctions for noncompliance.

Naturally the Act has caused some concern among the agencies. On the whole this is not because they object to showing an individual any credit rating they have on him, but because they are loath to open up to him the entire file, thereby revealing sources of the information. The result for them may well be a drying up of those sources, which would make their business almost impossible to run.

It is a mistake to suppose that those who have in the past been concerned with the activities of credit-reporting firms would like to see them abolished altogether. In 1976, when considering closing down the Register of County Court Judgments, the Lord Chancellor's department was rash enough to say that one reason for considering this measure was based on the Lord Chancellor's view that 'the existence of the register is an unnecessary invasion of the privacy of judgment debtors.' This argument is as hasty as it is misconceived. As Susan Marsden-Smedley of the Consumer Council wrote in its 1971 Newsletter:

Credit reporting agencies are regarded by the Consumer Council as an essential element in the modern credit system. Firms who grant credit must have a reliable means of checking credit records of potential customers. Indeed, because indiscriminate credit-granting clogs the courts with debt cases and causes social havoc in the families of persistent debtors, we go further and take the view that potential creditors have not merely a right but a duty to check on credit-worthiness before lending.

In the event, the Chancellor was persuaded to change his mind, but there is still likely to be some alteration in the running of the Register and this is causing anxiety among trade-protection societies. The proposed change, supposedly to cut down on expenditure, will mean that the onus will be on the creditor rather than the court to enforce judgment debts and there will be a longer delay before debtors are registered. This will increase the problems of agencies striving to give reliable ratings.

The credit enquiry is an area where the careless handling of confidential information can have disastrous consequences for an individual. How much more harm, therefore, can be inflicted by the deliberate manipulation of another's secrets. As far as the client is concerned, there is a danger that an unscrupulous private detective might gain access to, and use, information which is 'blackmail material'. This is a suggestion that has been made by Members of Parliament and others in the context of unauthorized acquisition by private detectives of criminal records, but in reality although information as to a past conviction might deprive a person of the chance of work (if revealed in a pre-employment check), there is very little evidence that private detectives use such intelligence for their own purposes. Private investigators who are sufficiently lacking in scruples to consider this sort of activity have their eyes fixed on a far richer target, a target which is corporate as opposed to individual.

Industrial espionage – the business of dealing in company secrets – is a lucrative profession. One firm of Italian private detectives was some years ago reported to have received £20,000 for one successful assignment. In America the menace of the commercial spy is, and has been for a long time, regarded as a major and very real threat by industry.

Some industries are particularly vulnerable to the threat of espionage, mainly those which are involved in expensive research programmes and/or are striving to achieve technical advances or original design. The electronic, photographic, chemical, cosmetic, aviation, car and fashion industries are among the chief targets of commercial spies, although firms from all areas of industry have secrets that they would not wish their competitors to get hold of. Within any such commercial organization, there are vast amounts of information which could be of use to a rival company, from details of company structure and management, merger plans and take-over bids, through the area of production costs, sources of raw materials and research findings, to information about advertising campaigns, marketing policy and intention, details of tenders and plans for future prices.

Any idea that industrial espionage is generally carried out by an unscrupulous private detective who breaks into an office building of the unfortunate company and rifles through the filing cabinets with his pencil torch, is misconceived. The vast majority of leakages of confidential information comes about in a much more mundane fashion. Indeed, in many cases, there may have been no actual 'leak' at all. For the private investigator (or for that matter anyone) who knows where to look, there is a veritable treasure-trove of information waiting to be discovered within the walls of public libraries and trade fairs, and within the covers of trade publications and annual reports of industrial companies. Quite unwittingly a firm can thus reveal details about its plans for expansion, marketing or development which may prove to be of great interest and advantage to a competitor. An equally straightforward and easy way of learning a few company secrets is simply by keeping an ear open for gossip exchanged between employees, especially on occasions when the alcohol is flowing.

It can thus be seen that difficulty arises in drawing a line between what can be regarded as legitimate competitive investigation and what must be condemned as industrial espionage. Some practices, such as obtaining confidential information by 'planting' a man on the inside of a firm or utilizing electronic listening devices, or the straightforward theft of documents, quite obviously constitute industrial espionage. Other methods are much more borderline. As private investigator Peter Heims explained, 'I personally ... would consider that it was competitive intelligence to follow a representative of a firm and report on the addresses he calls at. I would, however, feel that it was industrial espionage to try to get the representative drunk and then persuade him to give details of his firm's customers. I would accept instructions to maintain observation on a factory and report details of lorries going into the factory, etc. I would, however, consider it to be industrial espionage if I was required to go into the factory under a pretext and photograph various pieces of equipment.'

Possibly that line should be drawn when the intelligence work takes the form either of using positive deception or of making direct approaches to employees or agents of the competitor in order to gain information. The latter practice is one of the most common methods of industrial espionage. The approach may be to any one of a variety of people, and may involve bribery or the provision of other incentives to co-operation. Starting at the bottom of the scale, there is the cleaning lady who may be persuaded, for a small sum, to hand over the contents of the waste-paper baskets, or the junior typists who can see no harm in supplying a man who is willing to buy second-hand typewriter ribbons. Neither realizes just how revealing these seemingly useless articles might be to a rival firm. The increasingly wide-spread use of dictaphones by company staff provides yet another source of confidential information for the commercial spy who gets to know the audio secretaries, unless care is taken to wipe each tape after typing. The common factor in all these cases is that the 'leak' by the employee is usually inadvertent. Not realizing the value of the material she is supplying, a secretary may hand it over for a little extra money or as a favour to the recipient.

This can be illustrated by a much-quoted case in which a girl employee was asked to photocopy a few documents by the director of a small competing firm. When told the documents were kept in the safe the girl hesitated. The director, instead of offering her the £50 or £100 which might have overruled her conscience, made the mistake of offering £5,000. He thus showed the girl the true value of the information. She told her husband who contacted the employers, and thus the 'spy' was caught.

Disclosure of information by employees is not always inadvertent, however. Many instances have occurred of employees and ex-employees deliberately copying or removing company documents and attempting to sell them to rival firms. This is predominantly the domain of the amateur spy, and is perhaps best illustrated by the Merck case, reported in 1962, and described in Peter Hamilton's book *Espionage and Subversion in an Industrial Society*, 1967.

The case concerned the pharmaceutical industry and in particular a British subsidiary of the American company Merck. A rival firm in this country was contacted by a man who offered technical information for sale. The information related to the Merck subsidiary and the rival company immediately informed the victims who in turn informed the parent company. The result was that some senior employees flew from America to negotiate with the spy for the information. Because it was feared that the information might relate to a new drug which had cost a vast amount of money to develop, the employees were authorized to make an offer of up to £10,000 to the spy to buy back the secret. The company assumed that the confidential information had come into the possession of a professional spy group. In fact the seller was a disgruntled ex-employee who had been sacked. When asked how much he was prepared to accept for the invaluable information, he suggested £50 but was beaten down to £30. In addition, he received a prison sentence of six months for his pains.

Perhaps the most increasingly common method of gaining access to a rival company's secrets is to go straight to the men who possess the knowledge via the process of 'headhunting', known euphemistically as 'aggressive recruiting techniques'. This practice of 'poaching' the employees of a competitor may be carried out in different ways. A direct financial incentive in the form of an offer of a higher salary might achieve the desired results, but the headhunter runs the risk of facing a charge of procuring the employee to break the terms of his contract. Therefore a well-composed advertisement in the national press or a technical magazine, designed to attract a particular person by demanding his exact qualifications, is sometimes a safer and more favoured method.

Headhunting and the voluntary movement of experts to companies within a competitive industry has reached huge proportions at the present time due to the economic conditions prevailing. Owing to the limits imposed on wage rises by the

Government, one of the few ways to obtain a salary increase is to change jobs. This has led to more movement of labour within certain industries and has caused tremendous difficulties for companies who are losing some of their best experts along with some of their best secrets.

Firms can to some extent protect their business from the threat of headhunting by invoking the Common Law with regard to the protection of trade secrets or by inserting a convenant in the employee's contract against working for a competitor in the future, but such a clause must not act in restraint of trade and, in any case, very often the damage is done before legal proceedings can be taken.

The law in relation to industrial espionage in its more recognizable form, that is, the direct obtaining of company secrets by bribery, deception, infiltration or theft, is by no means so clear. It is popularly thought that industrial espionage is a criminal offence. In fact there is no crime of industrial espionage in English law, although on occasion newspapers, commentators and even members of the Judiciary have made the mistake of assuming that such an offence does exist. Industrial espionage quite often goes hand in hand with the use of technical devices by private detectives and, in the same way that the law has been unable to keep pace with the technological advances in that area, so it has failed to respond to the increasing menace of business spying.

Although industrial espionage is not in itself an offence, it often involves the commission of acts which do fall within the scope of the criminal law, for example theft, criminal damage or burglary. The problem that arises is that the value of the information stolen can only be measured by reference to the worth of the paper on which it is written, maybe two or three pence, and therefore the penalties imposed by the courts are correspondingly low. The reason why no account can be taken of the value of the trade secret written on that paper is that, technically, information cannot be stolen. The Theft Act, 1968, requires that the property in question must be taken with the intention of permanently depriving the owner of it. This intention is practically impossible to establish in relation to information which is usually either recorded in duplicate or recorded within the minds of one or more of the members of the victim company. Furthermore, information is not covered by the words 'intangible property' used in the Act.

An extension of this problem is created by the situation in which an employee, rather than an outsider, does the espionage. As long as he is legitimately employed there can be no question of trespass; as long as he copies the information rather than taking the document itself there can be no question of theft. He can thus cause his employers to lose thousands of pounds from the disclosure of its trade secrets to a rival and yet be unanswerable to the criminal law.

Companies are not completely without protection. There are a few laws that can be invoked in some circumstances, although they are rarely designed to deal with the problem of industrial espionage. The British Corruption Act, 1906, provides for a maximum penalty of £500 fine and/or imprisonment for two years, if the company can show that the source of the leak was a bribed employee. We have already looked at the operation of the Wireless and Telegraphy Acts in relation to the use of bugging devices, although the penalties in that case are far weaker.

Once again that controversial offence 'conspiracy' can be utilized in some circumstances to control the activities of industrial spies. In June 1971, two private detectives were found guilty of conspiracy to obtain confidential information by corrupt and other unlawful means and fined £100 and £500 respectively. In April 1975 an interesting new development in the field of industrial spying took place when three men appeared at the Central Criminal Court charged with conspiracy to defraud Rank Xerox by dishonestly appropriating or disclosing copies of extracts of Rank Xerox's plans. The Rank Xerox case is an important one, as the charge amounted to a hitherto unknown use of the offence of conspiracy to defraud. In the event, after two trials, the men charged, a clerk, a university graduate and a staff agency consultant, were acquitted. It is as yet uncertain, therefore, whether the offence charged will be successfully employed in the future. If it is, then it will constitute the nearest thing in this country to an offence of industrial espionage.

It remains somewhat anomalous that the person who steals £1,000 from a company safe should be guilty of an offence punishable by fine and/or imprisonment, while the person who copies a sheet of invaluable trade secrets should be guilty, at worst, of the tort of trespass or of breach of contract. The reason for this situation may lie partly in the attitude of the British public and British business towards the threat of the industrial spy.

Industrialists in this country do not appear to be greatly concerned about the threat of industrial espionage. There are two possible reasons for this: either the scale of commercial spying in this country is not such as to warrant pressure from companies to introduce legislation (and not such as to warrant their spending large funds on counter-espionage security); or industrialists are unaware of the scale of the problem and are complacent about the security of their own organizations.

In the United States, where the drug industry alone spends $300 million on research, the problem is treated very seriously. For many American firms, the provision of counter-espionage precautions is regarded as of equal importance to the provision of safeguards against theft and pilferage; but then there have been several spectacular and well-publicized cases of commercial spying, causing the victims losses of millions of dollars, to serve as a warning to American businessmen. One of the largest single losses caused to any company through industrial espionage was that suffered by the American Cyanamid Corporation, when the formula for its antibiotic, tetracyclin, was stolen and sold to Italian competitors. This theft cost American Cyanamid an estimated $100 million.

There is no doubt that we, in the United Kingdom, do not experience the problem of espionage to the same extent as the Americans, and that it is a relatively new development over here. In 1968, at the time of his Bill, Sir Edward (now Lord) Boyle said, 'I would agree that it is not yet a major problem in this country, though it would be a mistake to suppose that it was not a problem at all ... It is clearly something we should consider well in advance of its becoming a major issue.'

The question is whether it is now a 'major issue'. It is quite certain that there is much more espionage around than would appear from the handful of cases that have come before the public eye through the criminal courts. The reasons for this are obvious. Firstly, there is very high probability that a firm which has been the victim of industrial espionage will never know about it; the essence of espionage is that the spy is stealing something intangible, and often the first indication of it that a company might have is when a competitor comes up with an almost identical product. Even then the victim might well put it down to coincidence and bad luck. Secondly, companies that have lost confidential information are frequently unwilling to publicize the fact due to the lack of confidence that might ensue from a revelation of such a security breakdown. They will quite often buy back the information for a high price to avoid an embarrassing loss of secrets.

Peter Hamilton, in *Espionage and Subversion in an Industrial Society*, suggests that British business intelligence is conducted within certain bounds and within certain unwritten codes of conduct, outside which it is not 'cricket' to venture. This view is to a certain extent backed up by the few cases of industrial espionage that have come in front of the criminal courts. In nearly every one of these cases, most of which involved employees offering their own firms' secrets to a rival company, the competitor immediately informed the victim and a trap was laid. Of course this does not mean that *all* UK companies have such high ethical standards, but it gives an indication that some residue of the 'Gentleman's Agreement' attitude described by Mr Hamilton still remains. As he himself explains, however, 'The system only works with those who know the rules of the game. "Unsporting" Americans, for example, nourished in a hard school of cut-throat competition . . . may not, and may not wish to understand the niceties.'

It is true to say that one of the biggest threats in espionage terms is that from foreign competitors and governments, rather than British rivals; from countries such as Japan and the Iron Curtain countries, where espionage takes on more of a politico-economic aspect than a truly commercial one. Stephen Barlay in his book *Double Cross* points out the dangers to Britain of the policy of free movement of labour within the Common Market countries. 'In practice,' he says, the result is a natural flow of workers from areas of unemployment and lower pay towards the comparative Canaans. There is no reason to believe that it will be different with scientists, engineers and business executives. Landau [a private detective] in Brussels, two private detectives in Germany and now enquiry agents in London have told me that they already do 'preliminary searches' for European staff consultants who hope to start an eastward brain drain from Britain.

The American and Japanese influence on the conduct of business intelligence is growing, and this is indicated by the number of jobs received by private investigators relating to counter-espionage. The Younger Report referred to an investigator who said that he had handled about fifty cases involving industrial espionage in the years of 1969–70. I asked Vincent Carratu for his opinion on the amount of commercial spying in this country and he expressed the view that there was more around than people were aware of. 'At this particular moment,' he said, 'I have four cases pending that involve espionage. I reckon to get forty to fifty such cases every year.'

The final question is how far the private investigator is involved in the race for competitive intelligence which is accelerating every year. The private detective is traditionally regarded as a likely candidate for an industrial spy, but the truth is that his involvement is of a very fringe variety, mainly on the borderline between legitimate competition and unethical espionage. The Association of British Investigators opposes the carrying out of industrial espionage by its members, but under some circumstances, unless the investigator makes a very thorough check of the reasons behind an assignment, he may never know to what use the information he obtains is being put: it might be a perfectly innocent enquiry; it might on the other hand be a front for less legitimate activities. Of course there are some private detectives who are prepared to accept more or less any assignment and are not particular over the methods they use to achieve a result. The private detective who uses 'bugging' equipment will probably also carry out the occasional espionage job, either with or without the use of that equipment. *Chemical Engineering* of 25 April 1966 gave the following advice on 'How to Hire and Use a "Special" Investigator':

'There are available a number of reputable firms and individual investigators who can be hired to obtain a specific piece of information. Of course, their fees are relatively high and they should be used only in cases where quick, precise information is essential.'

The general view, however, seems to be that the private detective's place in the world of the industrial spy is to some extent exaggerated both by those within the profession and those outside who wish to sensationalize his role. The most common 'spies' by far are the typists, the switchboard operators, ex-employees who unwittingly (or occasionally deliberately) pass on snippets of information to outsiders. In the next category are some business and management consultancy agencies who have the ideal cover for probing into the background and work programme of employees. Here we find also the detective agencies who are prepared to dabble in the espionage world; but as Stephen Barlay explains in *Double Cross*, the really big pickings in the espionage field are left to the true professionals and international spy rings.

It was of those organizations – the true threat – that Sir Richard Powell spoke in 1967, when he was the director general of the Institute of Directors. He said,

There are certain organizations that have been set up to steal – that is not too strong a word – to steal the formulae and industrial secrets to sell to a big parent organization that exists in Switzerland to my certain knowledge, and there is another that exists in Tokyo as well, and they are prepared to suborn anybody in order to get this information which is worth many thousands of pounds. Ten years ago you never heard of industrial espionage in this country but now it is quite clear that it is something which has to be dealt with. It's a nuisance which we've got to try and get rid of.

Unfortunately for those investigators who are trying to improve the image of their profession, the public has always associated the activities of industrial spying with private detectives. We have seen, to an extent, that this is a misapprehension. The truth of the matter is that the private detective – a shady and indefinable figure in the minds of many people – has become something of a scapegoat for all kinds of dubious activities, some of which are rightly laid at his door and some of which are not. Thus when yet another impropriety is attributed to what was described by one leading Sunday newspaper as that 'unpleasant breed, the private detective', no one is too surprised.

On the other hand the public tend to be shocked and outraged by any report exposing the activities of private security companies. They do not, for example, expect their friendly neighbourhood security guard to have a criminal record for dishonesty. The reputation of the security industry is not, of course, unblemished. The proverbial copy-book has been blotted in several instances by the intrusion of security companies into areas regarded as too public or too political, and by the activities of those firms that are prepared to accept almost any assignment. But despite the fact that there is no control over the security industry, sections of Parliament and the press still contrive to be shocked when undesirable elements are found to be practising in security.

In 1973, an exposé by a Sunday newspaper revealed how a number of security men employed by the Gas Board to guard money had criminal records. In the March 1972 edition of *Police Review*, Chief Inspector Sydney Pleece wrote:

Whilst no empirical figures are available, the Metropolitan Police Crime Prevention Branch offered me an estimate that of about 150–200 medium to very small companies offering various security services in the Metropolis, some 30–40 *per cent* are to be regarded as dubious, either because the principals have criminal records or employ men with such records or because of limited ability, equipment or unsatisfactory selling methods.

Furthermore, the *News of the World*, reporting on 'The Scandal of the Slipshod Security Firms', described how a man with a criminal record for fraud and receiving stolen goods obtained employment with four different security firms. In every case he used phoney references and employment record. In every case he was allowed to start work straight away or within a couple of days.

Over the past few years several similar reports have hit the headlines, but perhaps the most disturbing of all was a case that came to the forefront in June 1976. The case involved the theft of over £2 million in British and foreign banknotes from

Heathrow Airport – a theft ranking with the Great Train Robbery in size of haul. The theft was reported to have been perpetrated by two men, one of whom, it seems, was dressed in the uniform of an American-based firm of security air couriers called Purolator Services, which carried out a lot of work at the airport. The man, together with his accomplice, is said to have visited three cargo strongrooms and asked for certain packages. The requisite documents were produced and the packages, containing the currency, handed over. The two men simply walked out and drove away. One man has already been tried and convicted of the theft. A second man, named by the police as being wanted for questioning in connection with the crime, was an employee of Purolator who fled abroad and is currently being held in Switzerland. The investigations into this man's background which naturally followed reports of the theft revealed that he had convictions for armed robbery, fraud, wounding a police officer and impeding the arrest of a murderer. He had been employed by Purolator for about one month.

Irrespective of any connection this security man may have had with the Heathrow theft, the fact remains that such a character was allowed to slip through the vetting system of a company which, although not a member of the BSIA, is no fly-by-night firm of dubious origins but a large and generally well-respected American company. The question of how such a mistake could be made, together with the whole problem of screening processes, will be discussed in the next chapter. Quite often it appears to be pressure of work and a commercial abhorrence of turning custom away which lead to a lapse in basic procedures. If the result might be a repetition of the Heathrow raid then it does not seem worth the risk.

It should at this point be said that it is not always wise to take the press treatment of the security industry at face value. As with every newsworthy topic, there is sometimes a tendency among journalists to exaggerate or sensationalize the problems of the detective and security professions. Quite often only one side of the story is told, leading to a degree of distortion. This is not an entirely bad thing, however, since a little bit of sensationalism is sometimes needed to awake the public to dangers which undoubtedly do exist, especially when it may be only the tip of the iceberg which ever actually comes to light.

Revelations about security guards with criminal records probably make the best newspaper material, but there are other practices among security companies which, although subject to less exposure by the media, are just as harmful to the reputation of the industry. There are problems in trying to find out about these practices, but most people in the 'know' admit that they go on. In the end, I enlisted the help of a friend in the security business who agreed to conduct me on what can only be described as a 'mystery tour of malpractice'. In so doing, he emphasized that I was going to see examples of the very small proportion of companies who, by their activities, bring disrepute to the whole industry.

We started our tour in a West London suburb. Stopping outside a new development of flats, my guide pointed out a sign which informed anyone who was interested that —— Security Company was guarding the site. In fact, there were no guards there at all. Now this is not a particularly unusual situation, because quite a number of security firms are willing to hire out their publicity boards to clients who cannot afford to pay for manned security. Whether or not this is an acceptable practice is open to dispute, but where it does become objectionable is when such a board is put up on premises in order to 'fulfil' an insurance requirement that the policy holder employ a security firm – in fact, the client is paying only for the name, not for the service. In this case, there is no question of any deception towards the client on the part of the security company; it is acting in collusion with, and on the instructions of, the customer. But if it has knowledge of the insurance requirements, which any good security company should, then in my view it is acting unethically.

The practice of putting up these bogus signs becomes more culpable, however, when it is for the purpose of deceiving the client rather than a third party. Further along the same road we stopped again. 'There used to be a similar board on this fence,' my guide informed me. 'The security firm's "brief" was to guard the flats until they were occupied,' He told me that it was not long before the local community realized that the guards were fictitious. In one week every window along one side of the building was smashed, and the next week, someone from the neighbouring site removed the sign from its place and put it on his own fence for a joke. There it stayed until the owners of the second site removed it, but it served as a good illustration of the number of times that particular security firm fulfilled its contract.

Our next call was at premises belonging to a well-known manufacturer of savoury snacks. In the dark, the lamp-lit guardsroom clearly revealed the presence of a uniformed security officer. He was alone. The 'brief' for the assignment specified the provision of three men every night, but his colleagues were probably many miles away satisfying (or partly satisfying) the demands of a completely different client. This sort of practice, known as 'double-shifting' in the industry, is not only unethical but probably illegal too under the Theft Act, 1968 – obtaining a pecuniary advantage and/or property by deception. There is no doubt where that pecuniary advantage goes if a security company is able to obtain payment twice over for using the same employees – or even three times over. I was told of one such case in which a security firm was under contract to supply a guard to each of three factories situated in close proximity to one another. In fact the firm used one guard for all three assignments. And if the client phoned up the premises and received no answer? The excuse was simply that the guard had been doing his rounds at the time of the call.

It is relatively easy, by taking a little trouble, to find out if a firm is (or is not) supplying *static* guards as agreed. It is far more difficult to check that mobile patrols are being carried out properly. A *News of the World* reporter described how he obtained a job with a security company, and was instructed by a director to make fewer calls at premises than were obligatory under the contract with the client. Out of the four patrols agreed with several clients, he made no more than three, and sometimes only one.

The above cases all highlight practices which go on in some firms with the knowledge and active encouragement of the management; the object is to meet demand by cutting corners and it is no doubt a profitable way of running a security business so long as it is not found out. These are activities which are confined to a small number of unscrupulous security bosses, but not necessarily confined to the small local firms who so often get the blame for bringing the industry into disrepute. Some of the guilty ones employ 100 men or more; they cannot be written off as insignificant.

Danger also lies in the possibility of criminals deliberately infiltrating security companies with a view to criminal activity. In relation to the well-publicized Heathrow raid, it has been suggested that the security man involved might have been 'planted' by an underworld gang, and on other occasions this has almost certainly been the case both in the private detective and the security professions. In their evidence to the Younger Committee, the Association of Chief Police Officers of England, Wales and Northern Ireland said, 'while many private enquiry agents and other institutions are reputable, it has been suspected from time to time that people with criminal records and intent are employed in the commercial field of investigation and security and that in some cases, they have taken employment with a view to obtaining and supplying information to the criminal associates.'

Peter Smith explained to me, 'While the possibility that criminals might infiltrate, or even set up their own security firms, troubles the authorities, the Home Office has been unwilling to act without statistical proof that this has happened. These hard facts we have been unable to supply.' Securicor and its fellow companies have been unable to convince the Government of the dangers, but perhaps I can conclude this chapter with one 'hard fact' that appeared in a national daily newspaper of 22 March 1966. The paper reported: 'Three men were jailed for a series of thefts in which the controller of a burglar alarm firm was handing over keys of alarms and doors for duplication.'

7. The Toothless Watchdogs

Who watches the watchers and investigates the investigators? This must be the question asked by many members of the public who read in their newspapers about dishonest security guards and unscrupulous private detectives. The legal controls on these persons, such as they are, have already been described. They do not amount to much. The piecemeal legislation is, in many cases, being used to curb activities which it was never intended to cover, and the penalties are accordingly often totally inadequate. The few laws which have been enacted to deal with a specific aspect of the security and detective industry, such as the Consumer Credit Act, the Guard Dogs Act and the Administration of Justice Act, have only touched the tip of the iceberg. None of them has hit directly at the problems highlighted in the preceding chapter, problems of people with criminal records finding their way into an industry which is concerned with the protection of property and the prevention of crime, of people with no training or experience being employed to do a job which requires a level of specialist knowledge, and of firms being slack in the standard of the service they offer.

We shall see that in nearly every European country, in most American States, and in a score of other foreign Statute Books, there is some sort of compulsory registration or licensing system for private detectives and/or security companies. Many of the controlling laws lay down minimum standards of training as well as a basic requirement of a clean record for all personnel.

In the United Kingdom, the only controls and standards that exist are those adopted voluntarily by detective and security firms. Self-imposed regulation can be achieved by internal company rules and policy, by membership of one or more of the associations which have been formed to promote better standards within the industry, or by a combination of both.

For a security firm to increase its business, it is essential that it should enjoy the confidence of its customers and it is therefore vital that it should have an effective vetting system to ensure that the men it employs are trustworthy and suitable. Employers are hampered by the fact that they do not have any official access to police records and therefore they can never be one hundred per cent sure that the man they are dealing with is not a crook. Of course they can reduce the chances to a minimum by various procedures. In most cases this consists of asking the applicant for the job to fill in a very detailed form, giving the *exact* dates of previous employment and the names of past employers. The details are then checked and the employers contacted for confirmation. If there are any gaps in the man's career that cannot be accounted for, or past employers who have gone bankrupt and cannot be traced, then the chances are that the application will be turned down. Group 4 rejects on average 95 per cent of all applicants, and similar claims are made by all the large companies. Of course no system is foolproof and it is inevitable that on occasion an applicant will slip through who turns out to be a security risk.

I spoke to the managing director of one security company who had experienced a failure of his vetting system on one occasion. The applicant had filled in the application form giving names of past employers, all in the hotel trade, and dates of employment. The company in question checked the references carefully and, on getting satisfactory replies, engaged the man. In fact, the employers with whom it had verified the details were all relatives of the applicant, and the managing director only found out about the man's past convictions through the lucky chance that one of his ex-policeman colleagues recognized the man.

There is another way for a crook who is determined to infiltrate a security company to avoid being 'found out' and it is a method that has been used on more than one occasion. It is very simple. The applicant merely gives, as his own, the name and address of a friend, together with the correct work-record of that friend. The trick can only be discovered by a personal visit to the given address (and a bit of luck!). This demonstrates how a full fingerprint and Criminal Records Office check is the only certain way of verification. The operations manager of a London security firm said that as far as he could tell, all his men had first-class backgrounds and records, 'but if a CRO check were to be carried out today on every employee ... Who knows?'

All the security chiefs I spoke to made the point that errors are bound to occur and even the police make occasional mistakes over their recruits. Furthermore, as Peter Smith of Securicor explained, 'it is not the man with the criminal record who is the biggest worry, because usually he will be found out before it is too late; the greatest danger comes from the employee with a spotless past who "turns bad" for one reason or another.' There is nothing that a firm can do about this except select men with apparently stable home backgrounds.

One difficulty that faces companies hiring out men to patrol offices, factories and other places, is how best to ensure that the job is being done honestly and effectively; it would be all too easy for a guard to slip home to a warm bed instead of carrying out his patrol duties. Firms which are concerned to uphold standards will take every available measure to safeguard against this. Such measures will usually include phone-in checks and reports. The most valuable watchdog in this context is the 'time-clock', a specially designed sealed clock which is carried by patrolling guards. It has to be turned at intervals by keys which are placed strategically around the premises. It is admitted that these measures are not infallible, that reports might be falsified and that time-clocks may be 'fiddled' if the guard makes a duplicate set of keys, so companies attempt to reduce the chances of 'cheating the system' by the appointment of supervisors to make spot-checks on employees to ensure that they are fulfilling their duties.

Apart from the selection and supervision of employees, the other main area in which the industry is concerned to raise standards is that of training. Naturally it is only firms of a substantial size that can afford to run their own internal training schemes. There is no standard form of training which is followed; indeed every company has its own ideas of the best way to prepare men for security work. Brinks-Mat, despite its American connections, has an English management which believes that there is no substitute for practical experience. Therefore new employees are sent to Ireland where they receive the minimum of theoretical teaching and the maximum of practical experience by riding 'in parallel' on the armoured cars. This means that they simply become an onlooker with the normal number of crew members, and it is hoped that in this way a newcomer will slip into the discipline of the job, appreciate the importance of rules which may seem unnecessary at first sight, and thus develop the 'sixth sense' of security which is vital.

Brinks-Mat is a company which concentrates its operations entirely in one field, the field of high-value security transport. Perhaps it is for this reason that its practical approach to training works effectively. But it would be wrong to assume that such a scheme would be adequate in all cases, especially where companies offer a wide range of security services. For this reason, the larger firms mostly have their own training schools. There was a time when Securicor's eccentric ex-chairman, Keith Erskine, in an effort to expand his company's operations, reputedly would hire an ex-policeman and send him off to open up a new branch office in another part of the country, equipped only with a desk and a telephone. Those days are past, according to Peter Smith, the present chairman and managing director, who described eight regional training schools that his company now runs to provide introductory, supervisory and management courses for employees.

Naturally all the top security firms maintain that their own training system is the best. One that is widely recognized as setting an example to the rest of the industry is the school run by Group 4, which has its headquarters near Broadway in the Cotswolds. Every new employee is required to undergo an induction course which may be either residential at Broadway or regional, under the instruction of trainers sent out from the headquarters and aided by audio-visual equipment. The course is comprehensive in content and the subjects covered include: the philosophy of security, security personnel vetting and training, security of premises, action at the scene of a crime, industrial espionage and sabotage, computer security, electronic security, fire prevention, legal powers, report writing, cash security and cash-carrying, retail security and the Laws of evidence and procedure. Most subjects involve practical as well as theoretical instruction. All employees are required to return for refresher courses at intervals, and any employee in line for promotion to a supervisory position must attend at Broadway for pre-promotional man-management studies.

The success of this particular training school can be evidenced by the fact that demand from people outside the company wishing to make use of the facilities has led Group 4 to extend the school. It is now open to United Kingdom industrial companies who employ their own 'in-house' guards, and to clients of the firm's international offices, as well as its own overseas subsidiaries.

Internal training schemes are confined to the large operators in the security industry. The second method of improving standards is through membership of one of the many professional bodies in the industry, of which mention has already been made. Such control can take two forms. Either the association in question lays down rules of membership and attempts to ensure that the required standards are complied with, or it establishes its own machinery for testing standards whereby failure debars membership. The objectives of all the main associations involved in this area are broadly the same and are concerned with improving the general state and image of the security profession and exercising some sort of supervisory function over members. However they all go about achieving these aims in different ways.

Private-detective agencies are generally run on a much smaller scale than security firms and internal training is both impractical and uneconomic. Attempts to put the work of investigation on a more professional footing, therefore, rely heavily on the activities of detective associations.

The Association of British Investigators has a code of ethics and a list of by-laws. Anyone wishing to join the ABI must fill in a detailed application form and swear an affidavit that the contents are true. He must supply the names of three persons, two from the legal profession, who are prepared to act as referees. The application then comes up before the Membership Selection Committee where the details are checked and a decision reached on whether to approve the application or not. At the present time, a criminal offence (except for minor infringements such as traffic offences) is a bar to admission to the Association, although there is a suggestion that this rule might be relaxed in certain cases.

Even if the Committee approves the application, the prospective member has then to pass an examination. This demands knowledge of the criminal and civil law and legal evidence and procedure. The ABI officially states that it is satisfied that the examination is sufficiently difficult to weed out unsuitable applicants and claims a 50 per cent failure rate, but some members felt strongly that the standard was not high enough and this eventually led to a breakaway group founding the Institute of Professional Investigators.

The Institute, which encourages membership from police and private detectives alike, has its own system of registration of investigators but its main concern is with improving the standards of the profession, and all the Fellows of the Institute must either sit an examination or write a thesis on an aspect of detective work. The emphasis of the organization is not only on the investigation but also on the business side of running an agency, and subjects to be taken include report writing and business administration as well as the necessary legal curriculum. The Institute offers correspondence courses, seminars and lectures as well as the opportunity for a successful candidate to put letters after his name.

Both the ABI and the IPI have a disciplinary machinery for dealing with complaints against its members. The ABI has a set of detailed rules governing the operation of its disciplinary committee which outline the form of procedure and evidence and the possible punishments on a finding of guilt – reprimand, suspension or expulsion.

The Association and the Institute are the private detective's answer to the General Medical Council and the Law Society. They represent a valiant effort to exercise some control over a profession that may not enjoy universal popularity but fulfils a necessary function. In the final analysis, however, its sanctions are meaningless, except that they constitute a step in the right direction. Of what good would it be if a doctor, expelled from the General Medical Council for unprofessional conduct or gross incompetence, were able to continue in practice as if nothing had happened?

The International Professional Security Association is open to all those who employ men or are themselves employed full-time in industrial and commercial security. Private detectives as well as security officers may become members of IPSA, so its membership of about 5,000 (including overseas associates) is the most widespread of all the Associations. But IPSA is chiefly an organization for individuals, and although security companies, or their controllers, can become associate members, its value lies mainly in the help and improvement it can lend to individual security officers and small security firms who have not the facilities to train their own men.

The aims of IPSA are similar to those of the ABI and the IPI. In 1968 it formed its own institute, the Institute of Industrial Security, whose members are required to pass an examination which involves, among other subjects, questions on crime prevention, alarm systems, fire prevention, theft, trespass, powers of arrest and search, evidence and procedure, reporting and industrial relations. There is also a correspondence course which is very widely used by members. Apart from the Institute, IPSA runs training courses in security at basic, intermediate and advanced standard. IPSA is registered with the Training Boards under the Industrial Training Act and most boards will recognize the cost of IPSA training for training grants.

IPSA has been criticized in the past for failing to insist on an adequate standard among members – their number alone makes this a difficult task – but Len Palmer, the national secretary of the Association, says, 'In order that we accept quality rather than quantity we have our own inspectorate whereby all applicants for associate membership are scrutinized thoroughly and in some cases the applicants are refused. We are the only professional body in this field which operates our own inspectorate.' The advantage of IPSA is that it actually provides the training facilities. Its weakness is that, despite the activities of the inspectorate, its members are not required to take advantage of the training and Institute courses that are available; and, of course, nobody is *required* to become a member of IPSA.

The British Security Industry Association, on the other hand, does lay down requirements which have to be fulfilled by member companies. A firm applying to join has to satisfy the Council of Management that, among other things, it is soundly and ethically managed and that it has adequate financial backing and insurance. Indeed, an applicant for membership must show a £20,000 turnover over the two preceding years, and a £50,000 turnover if applying for associate membership only. Perhaps the most significant requirement demanded by the BSIA is that which relates to the vetting of personnel: 'Applicants must satisfy the appropriate Committee and the Council that they operate an adequate screening system for all employees which must examine the employee's background for twenty years prior to applications for employment or back to school-leaving age, as part of a general policy of ensuring that their employees are of good character.' They are also required to have an after-care procedure to detect persons of bad character who might have slipped through the screening, and those who become security risks subsequently.

These are obviously the sort of standards that one would like to see applied to all security companies, and to detective agencies as well. The BSIA has further rules concerning training, but these are not so apparently effective owing to the use of the word 'adequate' to describe the necessary standards. It would seem to be of far greater value were the Association to establish more concrete guidelines in this respect. I put this to John Wheeler, the director general of the BSIA, who said, 'Although this may seem vague, the Council of the BSIA do in fact know what they consider to be adequate in the field in which the prospective member intends to practise ... but we want to avoid increasing bureaucracy and complexity by specifying the rules for each area of security training.' The wish to avoid bureaucracy is understandable, but I am by no means convinced that it compensates for the disadvantage of leaving the decision of whether a company has achieved the necessary standard to the Council which, after all, consists of representatives from the member companies.

As far as enforcement of its rules goes, the BSIA is in a similar position to the Association of British Investigators. Two years ago, in the *News of the World* story which highlighted the failure of certain security companies to vet prospective employees adequately, one of the firms named was AFA Minerva, a subsidiary of EMI Ltd. This firm had failed to check on the references of a man *before* they allowed him to start work. The man had in fact been to prison and the references were false. They were subsequently checked and he was dismissed immediately, but he had already been working for two weeks, which shows the danger of the 'start right away' approach adopted by some firms.

The alarm section of AFA Minerva is a member of the BSIA but, although this case in fact involved the guarding section, John Wheeler admitted that member companies are supposed to ensure that the spirit of the rule is observed throughout their organization. I asked him what action the BSIA will take in such cases and he explained, 'The attitude of the BSIA is that if the slip-up is merely due to incompetence and carelessness then no action will be taken. If the slip-up was wilful then the member will be pulled up in front of the Council and if the company does not intend to remedy the fault it will be thrown out of the Association.' A spokesman for AFA Minerva at the time of the incident was reported in the *News of the World* as saying: 'It is possible that our normal vetting system was not adhered to because of pressure to provide extra manpower, but this does not happen very often.' Small comfort, it would seem, to the client in this case. It is obviously essential that security companies should refuse work if they are unable to provide adequately screened guards. It is difficult to draw the line between carelessness and wilfulness in such a case, but then it is all too easy for the outsider to criticize the disciplinary measures of any association; it must equally be appreciated that the only way of improving standards within an association is by pressure exerted by fellow members. Expulsion does not solve anything.

The greatest weakness of the British Security Industry Association lies in the fact that, as John Wheeler himself has said, 'BSIA is as good as its membership wishes it to be and for some purposes its strength depends on which and how many companies seek to join it and participate in its development.' In fact, the Association's membership is numerically small, consisting to date of 51 associate and member companies, but it claims to represent 90 per cent by volume of the British security industry and says that companies are queuing up to join. The leading three or four guarding companies are all members, and indeed were closely concerned with the setting up of the Association. One of the earliest chairmen was Sir Philip Margetson of Securicor and the current chairman of the transport division is Peter Smith. Similarly J. A. Shepherd Brown of Security Express is the honorary treasurer and R. J. How of Chubb Wardens was the 1975/6 chairman of the Guard and Patrol Section.

Ninety per cent of the industry may seem like a large amount, but is it enough to give BSIA the right to claim to represent the whole industry, especially in view of the fact that the remaining 10 per cent probably includes something in the region of 700 firms? It would be wrong to jump to the conclusion that these firms are either all 'one-man bands' or all badly run. On the contrary, I was shown around a few very efficient companies, employing substantial numbers of men, which were not members of the BSIA. These firms were conscious of the need for careful vetting and training, but did not consider they would gain from membership of the BSIA.

Despite this, John Wheeler made it clear to me that one of the chief aims of the BSIA is to publicize their aims and standards in an effort to encourage customers to use only their members for security work. He was critical of the police force for not confining their recommendations to BSIA members. Alan Thomson, a chief superintendent in the Scotland Yard Crime Prevention Department, had this to say on that count: 'We always give a list of security companies that we recommend. They are not exclusively BSIA members because this is not always practical and there are good and reliable firms outside the Association. If we are asked to recommend a company in a rural area, for instance, which is not served directly by a BSIA member, we will suggest some local firms which we consider to be reliable.'

A similar problem can be found in the field of alarms. The National Supervisory Council for Intruder Alarms was set up

by the BSIA to encourage the intruder-alarm industry to cope
with the provision and maintenance of satisfactory alarm
systems in accordance with the British Standard for alarms,
BS 4737. The National Council is an extremely valuable organization which has undoubtedly contributed to the raising of
standards in the alarm industry. It has a band of inspectors
whose job is to ensure that member companies are complying
with BS 4737. The difficulty that once more arises is how far the
NSCIA is justified in encouraging industry to use only its own
members when there are many firms who, while they comply
with BS 4737, object for one reason or another to paying an
organization to check that fact. I have found some bitterness
among non-member security companies who have been refused
work on the ground that they are not NSCIA members, even
though they have tried to explain to the client that their
company does comply with the British Standard.

For what reason, therefore, does a reputable security
company (or for that matter a reputable private detective)
make a decision not to join an association which has been set up
in order to improve the image of his own profession? In talking
to various security firms, both association members and non-
members, a large variety of motives has been canvassed. A selection of these includes: that the BSIA consists of too many
vested interests; that the NSCIA demands unreasonable and
unnecessary details of an applicant's financial policy and position; that 'our own standards are good so why should we bother
about trying to improve everyone else's' (a rather insular attitude); and that there are members of the BSIA who should put
their own house in order first.

I asked John Wheeler for his view on why some good firms
chose to stay out of the BSIA or the NSCIA. 'Some have a
specific reason,' he said, 'such as a fundamental disagreement
with one of the basic principles of BSIA policy. Others may
decide not to join because of the subscription fee, even though
this is related to the size and turnover of the applicant. But quite
often it is simply a matter of personalities; X will not join because he does not get on with Y who is already a member.'

Similar problems exist in the private detective's profession.
Colin Findlay, the head of a well-known and well-respected

agency in London, is not a member of the Association of British Investigators. He feels that the ABI numbers too many ex-policemen among its ranks truly to represent a profession which deals with 99 per cent civil work, work which is often completely new ground to men leaving the police force.

Despite these difficulties, there have occasionally been suggestions from some associations that they should be directly involved in the regulation of their profession. As recently as last year, the ABI proposed that control should take the form of compulsory membership of their organization, but the idea has since been abandoned and the ABI now recognizes that an independent regulatory body is necessary.

The BSIA, too, while professing support for the principle of governmental control of the industry, has seemingly wavered when 'coming to the crunch' of how to set up such a scheme. In an article in the *Security Gazette* of June 1976, John Wheeler wrote, 'Should the licensing system be administered by the industry or by the central civil servants? It may be argued that many professional bodies in the United Kingdom essentially police and discipline themselves. Why should there be an exception for the security industry?' He concluded, '... in the final analysis, it will be for the industry itself to cast out from its ranks the less desirable elements in order to retain its integrity and the respect of the commercial, industrial and private clientele.'

With respect to Mr Wheeler, there seems little chance that the industry will ever be able, effectively, to rid itself of those undesirable elements. Both the security and detective industries differ from the other professions in that no qualifications are needed to practise in security, and consequently there is no examining body with a mandate to select its members. So when, in August 1975, in reply to a question on the security industry, the then Home Secretary Roy Jenkins said, '... as My Honourable Friend may know, the industry association concerned recognizes the importance of proper standards in this field and already operates a code of practice for its members', it must be said that this was a gross simplification of the real situation.

At the moment, the industry is fragmented, and what it needs is unity of thought over the improving of standards and an association or number of associations that can attract *all* the reputable security firms or private detectives into the fold and, at the same time, impose sufficiently defined rules so that any breach is apparent. At present, none of the associations provides all these requirements. While the situation remains in which there are good firms as well as bad operating outside the recognized associations, then expulsion can never be a really effective sanction for non-compliance with standards and regulations, and the professional associations will continue to be 'toothless watchdogs'.

8. At Home and Abroad

The fact that the 'toothless watchdogs' remain the only guardian of the public interest in relation to private security and detective firms does not mean that efforts have not been made to put the control on to a more official footing; and those working for reform in this country certainly have an abundance of foreign legislation on the subject from which to draw inspiration and ideas.

In Europe, the United States and other Western-style democracies there is to be found a variety of laws regulating most of the activities that have been discussed in this book. It is not true, of course, to say that each of these countries has legislation to cover every eventuality, but the majority of them provide some kind of control in one or more areas of private security or detection.

As far as the investigative profession is concerned, more attention is paid to its members in America than on this side of the Atlantic. Of the fifty federal States, thirty-five impose some sort of restriction on the operations of private-detective agencies. Most provinces in Canada and Australia also impose licensing for private detectives, as do Israel and New Zealand. The Private Investigators and Security Guards Act, 1974, of New Zealand is one of the newest pieces of legislation in this field and also one which is commonly cited as being an example that we, in the United Kingdom, should follow. As with many statutes regulating private police, this deals with both guarding and investigation in the one Act. In view of the difficulties of definition which are found in this context, it is worth while examining the definition of a private detective adopted in New Zealand, a country of similar society to the UK, and with basically the same legal system.

Section 3 of the Act provides that:

(1) In this Act 'private investigator' means a person who carries on any business, either by himself or in partnership with any other person, whereby:

(a) At the request of any person as a client of the business and not as a member of the public or of any section, and

(b) For valuable consideration, he seeks or obtains for any person or supplies to any person any information described in subsection (2) of this section.

(2) For the purpose of this section, 'information' means any information relating to:

(a) The personal character, actions or behaviour of any subject; or

(b) The financial position of any person; or

(c) The occupation or business of any person; or

(d) The identity or whereabouts of any person, but does not include information that is contained in a public record.

The important exclusions from this definition which are set out in Section 4 of the Act include, 'A person who seeks or obtains information for or supplies information to the Crown, or to a member of the Police, or to a local authority', and banks, credit bureaux, debt-collectors, journalists and process-servers are expressly not included in the definition of private investigator.

The form of control laid out in this statute is similar to that adopted in many American states. No person is allowed to be a private investigator unless he is the holder of a private-investigator's licence, and such a licence will not usually be granted unless the applicant is twenty years of age or over and has had at least twelve months' experience in the field for which he is applying to be licensed. It is a bar to the granting of a licence to have been convicted, within the ten years preceding the application, of a crime involving dishonesty, or to have had a licence or certificate of approval cancelled within the preceding five years.

A certificate of approval is the certificate which is granted to one who in New Zealand is known as a 'responsible employee' of a private detective. A licensed private detective is forbidden to employ any person on the actual detection side of his business who is not in possession of a certificate of approval issued by the regulating authority. Such a certificate will only be granted if the Registrar is satisfied that the applicant has complied with requirements and is a proper person to be a responsible employee.

In the case of both the licence and the certificate of approval, a copy of the application is sent to the police who may, within a certain time, file a notice of objection to the licence being granted. If there are objections from the police or (in the case of a licence) from any other persons, then there will be a hearing of the application for the licence or certificate of approval.

These, then, are the bones of the licensing system in New Zealand. Naturally there are many more provisions relating, amongst other things, to the bonding of licensed private detectives and to the disciplinary powers of the licensing authority in the event of a complaint against a private investigator, including the cancellation of the licence. It is a system with many attractive features, not least the requirement of a certain period of experience before licensing, although perhaps one of the omissions is the absence of any positive requirements for academic or examination qualifications.

In Europe, it seems that less concern is manifested over the control of the private detective himself, although there are laws governing certain of his activities. This is partly attributable to the fact that his role in Europe is less developed or accepted, certainly than in the United States, and possibly than in New Zealand as well. In Scandinavia, for example, the investigator has a small part to play in the structure of the society, especially when compared with the private security industry which plays an accepted role in crime prevention and is part of the fabric of the society. None of the Scandinavian countries have licensing laws for private detectives and neither have Belgium, Holland, France nor, of course, the United Kingdom.

Germany, on the other hand, does have a system of licensing for private detectives (perhaps more accurately a system of self-regulation) under the Code of Ethics and Articles of Association of the Central Association of Investigating and Detective Agencies. Spanish law lays down a complex proficiency test for persons practising as private detectives, but probably the most developed licensing system for investigators in Europe is to be found in Italy.

Under Italian law it is forbidden to provide services of surveillance or safeguarding of personal and real properties, to carry out investigations or enquiries, and to gather information on behalf of private individuals without the licence of a Prefect. In general, no licence can be granted to people not of Italian citizenship, not capable of being bonded, or having been convicted of a criminal offence. A further provision states that a licence will not be granted to persons who cannot show technical ability or qualifications for the services they wish to provide.

Two interesting features of the Italian legislation are, firstly, that an agency must keep a list of its current activities at all times, and show this to the police if requested to do so; and, secondly, that Surveillance and Private Investigation Officers are required on request to give their services to the police authority, and to comply with all requests addressed to them by police officers or bailiffs. Private detectives in Italy are thus technically auxiliary policemen.

In some respects, therefore, the European private eye, outside Italy, operates on a fairly loose rein. There is one law indirectly affecting the activities of the private investigator which is common to all European countries, that is the principle embodied in Article 8 of the European Convention on Human Rights which provides that: 'Everyone has the right to respect for his private and family life, his home and his correspondence.' The general concept of the protection of privacy is somewhat alien to the British constitution, but many European countries do in some way give force to this general principle of a right to privacy.

The protection of the right of the 'personality' (*Persönlichkeitsrecht*) is a fundamental principle of German law which is embodied in the Federal Constitution of 1949. Article 1(1) states: 'The dignity of man shall be inviolable. To respect and protect it shall be the duty of all state authorities,' and Article 2 provides that: 'Everyone shall have the right to the free development of his personality in so far as it does not infringe the rights of others or offend against constitutional order or the moral code.'

The Federal Supreme Court of Germany has developed a

right of the personality around these articles which is sometimes wider than the general right of privacy. Such case-law has its origins in the Schacht Case of 1954, in which a newspaper which portrayed a certain attorney in a false light was held to have infringed the right of the personality. The principle also offers protection, amongst other things, against the secret recording of conversations, and the unauthorized disclosure of confidential correspondence.

In France a similarly wide provision of the 'Code Civil' has been utilized to provide a general protection of privacy. Article 1382 states that: 'Any act of a person which causes damage or injury to another puts the person by whose fault it has occurred under an obligation to make amends for that damage or injury.'

Invasion of privacy is regarded as a 'fault' within the meaning of this Article, and on the basis of this principle, French law has developed certain rights of personality, being rights to honour, reputation, image and writing.

The Swedish Penal Code of 1962 protects an individual's right to privacy to a lesser extent by making the 'violation of the domicile' an offence (domicile here meaning a person's living quarters) and by embodying in law the right to secrecy of correspondence.

Right of privacy is recognized in the United States, although it varies from State to State. There are no definitive borderlines, but those formulated by Professor Prosser are widely accepted as being correct. He describes four different types of invasions protected by the concept of privacy. They are:

(a) Intrusion upon the Plaintiff's seclusion or solitude or into his private affairs;

(b) Public disclosure of embarrassing private facts about the Plaintiff;

(c) Publicity which places the Plaintiff in a false light in the public eye; and

(d) Appropriation for the Defendant's advantage of the Plaintiff's name or likeness.

A recent Bill put before Congress to extend the right of privacy proposes that private detectives should be under an obligation always to inform a subject that he, or she, is being investigated. This has, not unnaturally, caused widespread concern among American private detectives who fear, with some justification, that such a law would make their job virtually impossible.

European countries have not yet gone this far in controlling the activities of investigators, but the two areas in which there has been the most pressure to legislate (with varying degrees of success) are those of industrial espionage and the use of technical surveillance devices. Industrial espionage is the less well-covered of these two activities. In France, stealing of ideas is a tort but not a criminal offence; the law of 17 July 1970, although introducing increased protection against invasion of privacy, applies only to the individual and offers no remedy to commercial organizations suffering losses as a result of intrusion.

The German Penal Code contains a measure of protection in its paragraphs 299 and 300. The first provides that it shall be an offence for a person intentionally and without authority to open a sealed letter or other document which is not intended for his information, and paragraph 300 makes certain breaches of professional confidence criminal. Apart from these provisions, the Germans rely on a law of 1909 against unfair competition in which the betrayal of business secrets is made a civil offence and, although there is a new Bill proposed to deal with industrial malpractice, this again confines itself to creating civil remedies.

In much of Europe, the law against industrial spying is restricted to penalizing unauthorized disclosure by employees (like the English breach of confidence) and is not therefore equipped to deal with the activities of private detectives and spying organizations. Belgium, France, Italy, Sweden and Denmark have such legislation but, unlike this country, they impose criminal penalties for disclosure by employees. The Penal Code of Spain (Article 497) and the Civil Code of Holland (Sections 272 and 273) appear to offer more direct protection against industrial espionage, while Switzerland has a unique law against economic espionage which makes the theft of trade secrets for or on behalf of a foreign entity or concern, a crime.

As far as technical surveillance devices are concerned, the laws of other Western Democracies are far more specific and strict. In the chapter of their report dealing with surveillance devices, the Younger Committee examined closely the legislation proposed and operating in other European countries and in North America. Of the twelve countries studied (Austria, Belgium, Canada, Denmark, France, Germany, Holland, Italy, Norway, Sweden, Switzerland, USA), all had penal provisions relating to aural surveillance, with or without making a recording, except Canada, which had proposals for such legislation. In addition, France, Holland and Sweden were found to have penal enactments against visual surveillance, while Belgium and Denmark had proposals for similar legislation.

There was generally widespread prohibition on the disclosure to a third party of material gained by surveillance. Among these countries there is a division of opinion on whether the surveillance should be required to be surreptitious or whether mere lack of consent should suffice. Austria, Belgium, Denmark, Germany, Norway, Italy and Sweden reflect the latter view, while the United States, France, Holland and Switzerland follow the former line. Some of the countries involved have also enacted miscellaneous provisions relating to the manufacture and importation of such devices and regulating their possession and advertising as well.

The United States deserves some special attention in this respect. The use of bugging equipment, telephone taps and other unauthorized surveillance devices reached such epidemic proportions there in the late 1960s that America earned the nickname of the 'wire-tappers' paradise'. In an effort to combat this unwelcome and growing tendency, Title III of the Omnibus Crime Control and Safe Streets Act was passed in 1968. Its expressed purpose was to prohibit 'All wire-tapping and electronic surveillance by persons other than fully authorized law enforcement officials engaged in the investigation of specific types of major crimes after obtaining a court order ...' The most important provision in the Act is Section 2511(a), which states that any person 'who wilfully intercepts, endeavours to intercept, or procures any other person to intercept or endeavour to intercept any wire or oral communication ... shall be fined not more than $10,000 or imprisoned for not more than five years, or both.' The same Act also prohibits the manufacturing, assembling, possessing, selling or advertising of surveillance devices, with similar sanctions for contravention. These are very tough penalties, reflecting the concern felt in the United States for the bugging situation, and rather more realistic than the punishments at present meted out in this country.

As far as legislation which is directed specifically at the security industry is concerned, more attention in Europe has been generated in relation to private security firms than towards their counterparts in the detective profession. This is probably due to their very rapid expansion in numbers and to the important role they now play alongside regular police forces in the prevention of crime. In most European countries, apart from the United Kingdom, there is some sort of system of control. For example, in Italy, the same law governs security guards as private detectives and the appointment of security guards must be approved by the Prefect. There are certain basic qualifications laid down in the statute, but in addition there are two separate sorts of security guards in Italy: the so-called 'sworn guards' who are permitted to carry firearms and who perform the most dangerous tasks such as escorting cash, and other guards who are not 'sworn' and are not permitted to carry guns. It was estimated in 1976 that there were approximately 40,000 sworn guards and 484 security organizations in Italy, a country where crime (and consequently private security) is growing at a fantastic rate.

Germany has been experiencing some difficulty in achieving a satisfactory standard of security, especially in her factories and in industry generally. According to a report in *The Times* of 4 May 1976, works protection duties in large and small firms alike are still entrusted mainly to pensioners. In 1974, an attempt was made to improve the situation by the introduction of examination regulations for works protection staff by the Chambers of Industry and Commerce in Ludwigshafen and Munster, and since that time, the need to employ qualified people for security positions has been stressed by management and unions alike. *The Times* estimated that in 1975 there were 107,000 employees engaged in works protection, 55,000 of them being in-house personnel and the remainder contracted out from the 824 private security firms in Germany.

In the rest of Europe, and particularly in those countries closest to Great Britain, the most popular method of regulation has always been a system of certifying a clean record for prospective security employees, either by imposing the obligation on the employer (in a way similar to the New Zealand legislation reviewed earlier), or by putting the onus on the employee to obtain his own certificate. J. Philip-Sorenson of Group 4 is in favour of the latter approach because he believes it is a more acceptable way of checking on the past of an applicant for a job and that it involves less of an invasion of privacy. The system works by requiring every applicant to go along to his local police station for a certificate to say that he is a suitable candidate for the job. The police normally have a discretion, within certain guidelines, in what sort of convictions should be taken into account in making out the certificate. As Mr Philip-Sorenson explains, 'If the applicant does not return to the security company to which he has applied, then no one is any the wiser. He may have failed to get a certificate, or he may, on the other hand, have found another job.'

This system would seem to be one of the fairer ways of checking on the character of prospective security employees, and it would be a matter of further decision as to whether it should be operated within the provisions of the Rehabilitation of Offenders Act, and thus exclude from consideration convictions recorded over a certain period previously. It is a system which in essence is adopted in France and Belgium, and up to a short time ago in Sweden as well.

Sweden, however, has now gone further in control over private security companies by passing a new Act which has wide-ranging effect and imposes much more positive standards. It is an Act which will be of great interest to those in this country who wish to see more than a basic form of licensing involving little more than a check against criminal records.

The new licensing system imposes minimum standards of training for private security employees. It requires that every such employee should undergo a minimum of 214 hours of a training programme that must be approved by the Government. In addition there is a stipulation demanding refresher courses every year and 40 hours extra training for any specialist duty, such as handling guard dogs. The new Act limits the amount of overtime that any one employee can undertake in a year to 200 hours, a much needed regulation in an industry which often has its manpower stretched to cope with demand.

This Act, laying down strict and definite requirements of training, is the first of its kind, at least in Northern Europe, but in America there has for some time been pressure on States to legislate in this fashion, especially since the 1972 Rand Report, which was highly critical of American security organizations, and which detailed a variety of misdemeanours by untrained and unscreened private security personnel.

The situation at the moment is that thirty-two out of the fifty States have some form of regulation over guard and patrol services. Of these, twenty-nine run a criminal record check and/or require the applicant to be of good character, twenty-five Only fourteen States actually require the prospective licensee to take a written examination, and very few lay down the sort of training that the applicant must undergo.

There is likely to be some change in the regulation of the security industry in the United States, however, in view of the Government Committee – The National Advisory Committee on Criminal Justice Standards and Goals – which has just issued a 500-page report on the security industry, containing recommendations as to its future conduct and regulation.

The report opens by acknowledging that the enormous growth in the security industry means that it constitutes a massive and valuable resource for the prevention of crime, but it also states:

This significant growth has not been accompanied by a growth in measures devoted to evaluating and upgrading the security industry in relation to its efficiency and effectiveness. The security industry is plagued by a variety of potential and actual problems, including low wages, poorly qualified and untrained personnel, abuse of local authority, lack of regulation, and excessive false alarms, to name but a few.

The most important recommendation to remedy this situation made by the Committee is that there should be regulation at a State level, to be achieved by the setting up of a regulatory board in each State. The report proposes that all commercial demand a period of security-related experience before licensing.

security and detective organizations should be licensed. Applications for a licence would have to contain certain information, and all applicants would be required to name one individual to act as a 'qualifying agent'. The person named would have to meet certain qualifications, including a requirement of experience in some area of security.

Only commercial security firms would be licensed under these proposals, but the report recommends that *all* persons engaged in security functions should undergo registration, thus bringing in-house personnel under the control of the State. The Committee rejected calls for the exemption of proprietory (in-house) security organizations on the ground that, 'The potential threat to the public from abuses of authority, such as assault, unnecessary use of force, false imprisonment or arrest, improper search and interrogation, impersonation of police officers, and mishandling of weapons, is just as likely to occur with proprietory personnel as with contract personnel.'

Qualifications for registration are at two levels, depending on whether the applicant is to be armed or unarmed; the latter is naturally less stringent. The most interesting aspect of the report, in my view, is that it proposes minimum training requirements for all personnel, armed and unarmed, and it lays down very definite guidelines as to the form that training should take. It recommends that every security employee, including investigators, guards, watchmen, armoured-car personnel, couriers, alarm-system installers and servicers, and alarm respondents, should have a minimum of eight hours pre-assignment training and, during the first three months of employment, be required to complete a basic training course of thirty-two hours. The report outlines in detail the proposed contents of these courses. In addition, armed security personnel would have to undergo successfully a twenty-four-hour firearms course and would be required to requalify at least once every twelve months.

Although neither policemen nor security men are armed in the United Kingdom, in the rest of Europe the arming of private security personnel does take place, but on a more limited scale than in the United States. France is probably the closest to America in this respect, with arming generally, within the overall control of the French licensing system. Other countries, such as Belgium, Norway and Sweden, permit private security guards to be armed only in certain areas of work, normally cash-carrying, and sometimes only for cash runs involving particular risk. In Sweden, for example, a very small proportion (about 2 per cent) of security men are armed, and permission to arm is given under strict control. Security guards who are armed have to wear a special gold insignia and they come under direct police supervision. In Belgium, security men who carry arms have to possess a certificate of proficiency.

In this country, fortunately, the problem of training security men in the use of firearms is not with us since the private security industry is, and seems likely to remain, prohibited from carrying guns. However, having reviewed generally the legislation in relation to private security companies and private detectives in many countries in the world, it is apparent that either the United Kingdom does not experience the same problems in relation to the industry as other countries (which seems unlikely), or we are dragging behind the rest of the world in respect of our controls over private police.

There has over the last decade been mounting pressure on consecutive Governments to legislate in this area. It would be true to say that rather more of this pressure has been directed towards controlling private detectives than towards security companies. Anxiety over the latter is of a more sporadic nature, manifesting itself at intervals whenever a particularly worrying story hits the headlines, such as the guarding of immigrant deportees by private guards or the intervention of a private security company in the Hornsey Art College student troubles. More recently, after the £2 million raid at Heathrow Airport, the *Daily Telegraph* reported, 'The Government is expected to come under renewed pressure to introduce a system of compulsory registrations for security firms and to improve facilities for firms when checking on the background of potential employees.' But the result of any such pressure was negligible and now the storm has blown over once more.

The activities of private detectives have come more regularly under review in Parliament and elsewhere, usually in the context of the controversial question of the invasion of privacy. In

Paragraph 445 of the Younger Committee Report on Privacy, it was said, 'The work of private detectives is of exceptional concern to us because invasion of privacy is the essence of it.' It is against this background that many of the attempts to control private detectives must be considered. Proposals have come in many different forms; some have been intended to serve as a general protection against the invasion of privacy, while others have been directed specifically at controlling private detectives or their activities.

The earliest Bill of its kind was the Right of Privacy Bill, which was introduced in the House of Lords by Lord Mancroft in 1961 and this was followed, in 1967, by another Bill on the same subject presented, this time in the House of Commons, by Alexander Lyon, MP. Neither of these Bills attracted a great deal of publicity and both failed to become law.

The next move towards control was centred around a particular activity, namely industrial espionage. Industrial espionage had been touched on in the Lyon Privacy Bill and was also to be later covered by Brian Walden's proposals, but the Industrial Information Bill, presented by Sir Edward Boyle in 1968, represents the only attempt aimed specifically at rooting out industrial spying. Section 1 of the Bill ran as follows:

A person shall be guilty of the offence of misappropriation of industrial information as hereinafter defined who, without the consent of the rightful owner and possessor thereof:

(a) reads, copies, receives or records such information with any photographic and/or electronic device, or

(b) obtains such information from any computer, data bank, memory code, laser beam, satellite or from any cable telephonic or television system.

The Bill was adjourned on the second reading and did not become law.

In the year of 1969, two Members of Parliament took up the fight against the abuse of privacy. The first, Mr Anthony Gardner, directed his Bill (the original draft of which had been prepared by Peter Heims of the ABI) towards setting up a licensing system for private detectives. Section 1 provided: 'After the passing of this Act no person shall act as a private detective or investigator unless he has been authorized so to act by a certificate in writing under the hand of a County Court judge in the district where he is resident or has his place of business.'

One of the specific responsibilities of the Court would have been to satisfy itself that the applicant did not have his name recorded in any Criminal Record Office. The applicant was also to furnish to the Court a bond in the sum of £1,000. Under the Bill it would have been an offence to advertise as a private detective if not in possession of a certificate and the Court would have had the power to revoke the certificate or refuse to renew it if the holder abused his position. The Bill, which was introduced under the 'ten minute rule', failed to get a second reading, but it probably contributed to the Government's decision to set up a committee to look into privacy, with specific reference to 'intrusion by private persons and organizations'.

The second Bill of 1969 was sponsored by Mr Brian Walden, MP, and, although it was not specifically directed against private detectives, he made it clear in the debate that they were one of the main sources of anxiety that led him to introduce the Bill. He was particularly troubled by the use of certain mechanical devices, for example, bugging devices, either for industrial espionage or for collecting evidence against individuals. His concern also sprang from the activities of credit-rating agencies, especially in view of the tendency to centralize personal information in data banks and computers. The Bill defined the right of privacy as:

The right of any person to be protected from intrusion upon himself, his home, his family, his relationships and communications with others, his property and his business affairs, including intrusion by:

(a) spying, prying, watching, besetting;
(b) the unauthorized overhearing or recording of spoken words;
(c) the unauthorized making of visual images;
(d) the unauthorized reading or copying of documents;
(e) the unauthorized use or disclosure of confidential information or facts (including his name, identity or likeness) calculated to cause him distress, annoyance or embarrassment or to place him in a false light;
(f) the unauthorized appropriation of his name, identity or likeness to another's gain.

This definition of privacy can be seen to relate strongly to the activities of private detectives, although one possible 'defence' was to be that the defendant's acts were 'reasonable and necessary for the protection of the person, property or lawful business of himself or any other person for whose benefit and on whose instructions he committed the infringement', a defence that could be cited by a legitimate private detective.

Mr Walden's Bill attracted much criticism, much support, but above all much publicity, and eventually at the end of the second reading on 23 January 1970, Mr Callaghan intervened and announced that the Government would set up a Committee to look into the privacy question. This all-important Committee, chaired by Sir Kenneth Younger, effectively put a stop to the clamour for control over private detectives. Although, in the meantime, 'Justice' issued its report 'Privacy and the Law', advocating a general right of privacy and control over the use of electronic surveillance devices, on the whole, people were putting their faith in the Government Committee. In July 1972, it issued its report containing the following proposals relevant to private detectives and their activities.

Briefly, the majority of Committee rejected the idea of a general right of privacy but recommended the setting up of a licensing system for private detectives, by which anyone wishing to practise in this capacity would have to obtain a licence, failure to do so amounting to a criminal offence. The purpose of the system would be to ensure the exclusion of persons known to be unsuitable to carry out the work of private investigation, for example those with criminal records of a relevant nature. The Committee had difficulty in deciding which would be the most satisfactory body to control the issuing of licences. It was finally decided that, ideally, an independent licensing authority would be the best solution, but failing this, the magistrate courts in England and Wales and the licensing courts in Scotland should act in this capacity. The suggestion that the police should serve as the licensing body was dismissed for reasons that will be explained later.

As was to be expected, the Committee was not satisfied with the situation regarding technical devices and recommended the introduction of legislation making it unlawful to use any electronic or optical device for the purpose of rendering ineffective as protection against being heard or observed, circumstances in which, were it not for the use of the device, another person would be justified in believing that he had protected himself or his possessions from surveillance whether by overhearing or observation.

Where done surreptitiously, it was proposed that such behaviour should constitute a criminal offence and a new tort of unlawful surveillance should also be constituted along with provisions relating to the advertising of devices.

On the question of industrial espionage, the Younger Committee reviewed the efficacy of the Industrial Information Bill of Edward Boyle, but they considered that it was unsatisfactory in its definition of 'misappropriation of industrial information'. They concluded 'that there would be difficulties of enforcement, mainly due to the reluctance of companies to report suspected offences, and that the penalties would be inadequate in view of the rich rewards which sometimes accrue from a successful operation'. For these reasons, the Younger Report did not recommend the introduction of a criminal offence to cover industrial espionage. Instead they proposed increased use of the civil law relating to breach of confidence and the introduction of a new tort of disclosure or other use of unlawfully acquired information. Together with the proposals on the use of technical surveillance devices, the Committee felt that these measures would deal adequately with the situation.

The Younger Committee Report met with a variety of reactions. There was widespread relief that positive steps had at last been taken, welcome for the proposals, and an urging that the Government put them into effect as soon as possible. A few bodies felt that the Committee had not gone far enough in their recommendations, while others were dubious as to the possible effects of the proposed system.

The *Guardian*, commenting on the law after the Court of Appeal decision in the Withers case, called for much sterner measures to prevent malpractices, including, in addition to a licensing system, a compulsory register of all cases being examined by private detectives to enable a supervisory body to scrutinize them and give directions as to what constitutes improper working practice.

The Association of British Investigators felt that the Committee should have gone further in a completely different way. Mr Philip Crofts, a member, expressed their view thus: 'The licence should also be a certificate of competency . . . The applicants should be carefully vetted before being licensed but *then* they should have more power than ordinary private individuals especially when serving processes.'

The members of the ABI, who have always favoured a licensing system, reacted particularly strongly to the suggestion by the Younger Committee that any licence should be overprinted to the effect that the private detective had no official authority and that there was no obligation to co-operate. Naturally, the ABI could see this acting as an impediment to public co-operation which, at the best of times, is not good. However, the proposal was included to pacify those quarters which feared that the issuing of a licence to each investigator might mislead the public into a false impression of his status. Opposition on this front came particularly from the police and also caused anxiety in Government ranks. Therefore, while the ABI likened the proposal to a dog licence, the Government regarded it in the light of a 'licence to pry'.

It was this consideration which persuaded the Government to oppose the recommendations of the Younger Committee relating to private detectives when they were finally debated a year later. The only concession made by the Home Secretary was the suggestion that a 'Disqualification Scheme' might be introduced by which anyone wishing to practise as a private detective would have to go to his local police station for a criminal record check which, if it proved positive, would disqualify him from practising. This is a scheme which bears some resemblance to the Continental approach and, although it represents the very minimum form of checking, it would at least be a step in the right direction. As yet, however, nothing has been done by the Government to implement this proposal.

The struggle continues. In 1974, Michael Fidler, MP, sponsored two Bills for the licensing of private detectives, both of which fell by the wayside, and there are several more proposals still at the drawing-board stage. But some campaigners for the control of investigators are beginning to lose heart, as the memory of a Government Committee who recommended their licensing fades further away.

There has not been quite such concentrated activity with regard to the control of private security companies and personnel. Indeed, until 1977, there had been only one legislative attempt, embodied in Member of Parliament Mr Norman Fowler's Security Industry Licensing Bill of 1973. Mr Fowler is on the Board of Directors of Group 4, one of the companies most concerned with the state of the industry today, and consequently he is himself involved in the fight for some sort of control. The Bill never reached the stage of specifying the system of licensing which it would set up – it was lost in the same way as most Private Member's Bills are. Mr Fowler's real intention in presenting the Bill was to draw the public eye and the attention of his colleagues towards the problem. In his opening speech on the Bill on 4 July 1973, he gave his own illustration of the urgency of the situation with a case which was first reported on the television programme 'This Week'. It involved a security company run by a man who admitted he had twice been convicted of grievous bodily harm and who employed four or five members of staff with criminal records, including one who had served sentences of three and five years for burglary and receiving. Any impression which this worrying tale made on the assembled Members was not enough to gain sufficient support for the Bill.

Recently there has been a renewed attempt to convince the Government and the Home Office of the need for licensing, and this attempt has come from Mr Bruce George, MP, in the form of his Private Security (Registration) Bill, 1977. The importance of this Bill is that, for the first time (apart from Norman Fowler's Bill which was never formulated), proposals for the control of both private detectives and security companies and their employees are embodied in the same instrument. In fact, the Bill covers practically every aspect of security, including guard and patrol services, security consultants, private investigators, armoured-car and courier services, services related to the provision of safes, locks and alarms and also proprietary or in-house security personnel.

The purpose of the Bill is to provide for the licensing of all commercial firms and individuals who offer such security services for hire or reward, and to set up an independent body (the Private Security Registration Council) to administer the scheme. This body will have the responsibility of dealing with all applications for registration and will have access to certain information, including criminal records. It will issue licences and/or identity cards where applications are approved.

Paragraph 7 of the Bill provides that: 'Licence applications shall include sufficient information about the applicant to enable the Council to determine if ethical, competent and responsible services can be provided.' This information will include, *inter alia*, a summary of the applicant's experience and training in security, and the name of a bank where he has been known for ten years.

Where the applicant for a licence is a corporation or partnership or an association of persons, strict conditions are laid down for the issuing of licences; for example, the demonstration of adequate training and refresher training programmes and supervision, the demonstration of adequate selection and vetting procedures, and the demonstration of adequate insurance cover.

Paragraph 15 goes further, in specifying that certain kinds of security personnel shall be required to complete a minimum period of pre-assignment training, a basic training course, and refresher training, although the actual period is left to be determined by the Council.

Inevitably, some criticism has already been levelled at the Bill. It has been said that although the Bill provides for compulsory training for, among others, private detectives and security guards, it does not differentiate sufficiently between the kind of training needed by those two groups. One or two weeks' basic training may indeed be adequate for certain guarding jobs. It is argued, however, that private investigators should serve an apprenticeship in the field as is required in some states of America.

A more obvious weakness of the Bill in its present form is the ambiguity that surrounds the actual procedure for applying for licences, as between employees and employers. From a personal point of view, my main criticism of the Bill is that it appears to have rejected the idea of the prospective employee getting his own 'clean bill of health' from his local police, before applying to be licensed or registered as a security employee; it seems to have opted for a process of application via the employer.

The Bill is as yet in its infancy, however, and there is plenty of time in which to remedy its teething troubles. What is important is that it is a step in the right direction. Bruce George has no illusions about the chances of success of his proposals. Once again they are presented in the form of a Private Member's Bill, and he knows that in the present climate of legislative pressure there is little possibility of their becoming law. His intention is to gain publicity and support in the hope of being able to introduce a similar Bill successfully in the not too distant future.

If that is to be achieved, his main energies must be directed towards persuading the Home Office of the need for licensing. To date, the Home Office has been reluctant to act without more proof of that need. In the House of Commons (House of Commons Reports, Volume 935, No. 136), Bruce George brought a few of his own illustrations with him; an armoured-car guard who aided a gang to a successful ambush of his security van worth £10,000; an employee of a security company who, whilst on his rounds silencing false alarms, used to help himself to the goods they were protecting; another security employee who burnt down a factory, causing £130,000 worth of damage.

One wonders what proof the Home Office requires. There will obviously have to be a few more £2 million raids at Heathrow Airport, before the authorities will sit up and listen.

9. Private and Public Police: Confrontation or Co-operation

Among the various quarters of the police force there have always been widely differing views of the private security and detective professions. Ten years ago the attitude of most policemen was, at best, one of unwilling tolerance and, at worst, one of suspicion and mistrust. The situation with regard to private detectives has changed little. Apart from the really professional agencies, the fraternity of private investigators is not looked on with very much fondness by members of the police. The attitude towards the role of the security company has changed, however, and it is continuing to change. The main reason for this is that an approximately 35 per cent crime-detection rate has driven home to many policemen the fact that a policy of detection alone may not be enough; that prevention may be as necessary as cure.

The concept of crime prevention as a function of the police force first gathered momentum in the 1950s, and the Cornish Report early in that decade laid down the foundations of crime prevention in this country. In 1962, formal training in this new aspect of policing was begun, leading to the establishment of the Stafford Police College crime-prevention course and the setting up of local crime-prevention units all over the country. The importance of this development in Police and Home Office thinking is that the security industry is starting to adopt a recognized role in the practice of crime prevention.

This recognition is as yet limited and one of the problems for the police in recent years has been to tread the narrow line between offering too much or too little co-operation to the security industry; they have been accused of both at one time or another.

The question of co-operation has always been an emotive one, both in regard to private detectives and security companies. The reason for this is the movement of retired and ex-policemen into the private sector, either as directors or advisers on the boards of large security firms, or into the business of private detection. This has led to concern in the past over the possibility that information, particularly on criminal records, was filtering through an 'old-boy' network to ex-colleagues in the private sector. In 1968, Mr Anthony Gardner sought an assurance in the House of Commons that neither the police nor any other public body would provide confidential information about individuals to private detectives. The reply on behalf of the Home Office was as follows:

The provision of information from Police Records is essentially at the discretion of the Chief Officers of individual forces. For example, details of traffic accidents are regularly given to parties in civil cases, but other information required by public bodies for their public purposes *is not and cannot possibly* [my emphasis] be divulged by the police forces corporately or by individual officers of the court.

A forceful denial indeed, but reports of such disclosures have continued to filter back, and mention has already been made of the many prosecutions which have been brought against private detectives who managed to gain information of criminal records by deception. Moreover, it is not necessarily true that the only way that such information can be obtained is by the use of friendship or of deception. Stephen Barlay, in *Double Cross*, alleges, 'The truth is that any private inquiry agent worth his shoe leather, rich enough to pay his telephone bill, and smart is the name of the game, and has inside contacts. Yes, bribery is the name of the game, and in most cases the ultimate recipient is a policeman.' During the debate in the House of Lords on the Younger Report, Lord Gardiner said of private detectives: 'Many of them were openly saying that they could obtain anybody's criminal record from the Criminal Records Office for about £7.'

In April 1974, the British Legal Association was so concerned with the situation that it presented a report to the Home Secretary. Mr Jeffrey Gordon, chairman of the Association representing 3,000 solicitors, was reported as saying, 'Pernicious back-stage snooping and the development of bugging devices are on the increase, and we are particularly appalled by the possibility that men who have led a blameless life for, say, 25 years can be suddenly pushed back into disgrace by unnecessary and unfair disclosure of a conviction in their youth.'

The leakage of official records is of greatest concern when private investigators are involved, because on most occasions the information is for transference to a client. There is no doubt, however, that similar exchanges of information have occurred between the police and security firms, through senior ex-police officers employed by the companies. Not so long ago, access to criminal record information through contacts in the Force, while strictly unofficial, was certainly widespread. In the case of security firms, such information is not, of course, generally for transmission to others, it is merely to assist in efforts to ensure the honesty of employees. But the anxiety of the public is caused, not by the motive for the disclosures, but by the fact that they go on at all.

Unauthorized disclosures do still take place. I have met several private detectives who have no difficulty even now in obtaining the information they need, but it is no longer true that every private detective has his contact, and the flow of data to the security industry has been stemmed to a great extent. Indeed the instances of 'leaks' have been quite significantly reduced for two main reasons: firstly, the determined work of Sir Robert Mark to uncover officers breaching regulations and, secondly, and more important, the introduction of the Rehabilitation of Offenders Act, 1975.

The Act provides that:

Any person, who, in the course of his official duties, has or at any time has had custody of or access to any official records or the information contained therein, shall be guilty of an offence if, knowing or having reasonable cause to suspect that any specified information he has obtained in the course of those duties is specified information, he discloses it otherwise than in the course of those duties to another person.

This provision only applies to 'specified information' which is information about a 'spent conviction'. The effect of this provision is to turn what was once a mere internal disciplinary matter into a criminal offence, punishable by a £200 fine. Many people in the security and detection professions feel that this legislation holds serious consequences for their businesses.

Naturally it was necessary that disclosure to certain bodies should be exempt from liability under the Act, and some representatives of the security industry campaigned to be included among those exempted on the ground that access to criminal records was essential for the safe screening of security personnel. The argument put forward by representatives of the industry was, and is, that, while humanity dictates that a man should have a second chance and not be held responsible for the rest of his life for some folly committed in his youth, it also says that the same man, however straight the life he now leads, should not be exposed to unnecessary temptation. Temptation is something that the security industry can offer in abundance.

This claim for special treatment was nevertheless ignored by the Home Office. The reasons for refusing the security industry exemption from the Act were not made clear, but it must be assumed that it was the danger of abuse of the privilege that was foremost in the minds of the police and others. It would be possible, for instance, for a security company or private detective running a guard division to take advantage of the facility for checking records at the Criminal Records Office by conducting pre-employment checks on behalf of clients, or for the private investigator to use it as a short cut in other enquiries. A signed declaration of consent by the prospective security employee, or a system of disqualification as described earlier, might go some way to defeating these problems, but the decision of the authorities to refuse exemption in the circumstances serves to demonstrate that, while the security industry is now regarded as having a part to play in crime prevention, the authorities are still unwilling to make any effort towards materially improving the standard of the industry.

The same can be said of their attitude to private detectives. The police do not acknowledge the role of private investigators to the same extent as security companies, but they are only too aware that the presence of criminal elements in the detective profession can have as worrying consequences as in the security industry. The investigator, by the very nature of his work, is bound to be employed in order to gain information or evidence which in the normal course of things would be difficult to obtain. It may be information on Mr X's financial position or evidence as to Mrs Y's adultery. The enquiries would in all probability be perfectly legitimate, but nevertheless it is inevitable that the private detectives will become possessed of knowledge that Mr X and Mrs Y would not wish to be publicized. He will also become familiar with the running of certain businesses, banks, local authority offices and Government departments, their practices and procedures. The consequences of these two situations are obvious. The investigator has at once (a) potential blackmailing material, and (b) potential access to confidential information by adopting procedures he knows to be customary and therefore likely to convince an official of his authenticity. Actual instances where this has happened have already been described.

Despite this, the police did not give total support to the Younger Committee's recommendations on licensing. The Chief Officers of Police stated that they did not believe that there was a need for special control over private detectives (see Paragraph 461 of the Younger Report). This, in my view, springs more from a fear that issuing licences to investigators would give them an air of officialdom which could mislead the public, than from a genuine confidence in the law as it now stands. The view expressed is by no means a unanimous one amongst members of the police force, and the personal view of many is that they should be licensed. Some police, however, undoubtedly see licensing as the first step towards the 'official private detective' who, in America, is possessed of more powers than the private citizen and works in fairly close association with the police. A police force that regards the private detective as a 'necessary evil' is hardly likely to welcome such a situation.

The police also rejected the suggestion that they should act as a licensing body. The fear that this would inevitably involve them in checks at the Criminal Records Office probably has something to do with their reluctance to support the scheme. This is understandable in view of the manpower shortage which is already stretching them to the limit. The suggestion has been made that the CRO should be manned by civilians to defeat this problem, and that security companies and private detectives should have to pay for CRO 'clearance' in the event of licensing. It has even been estimated that the CRO could be run at a profit in these circumstances!

There is another reason why the police themselves should not be concerned in the actual granting of licences, however, and this was explained by the Younger Committee in Paragraph 461 of their report: '. . . it would be open to obvious objections if it could be said that the former colleagues of applicants for licences were in a position to decide that ex-police officers, rather than their competitors of other origins, should be the ones to get the licences.'

In any event, some policemen are still mistrustful of a licensing system. Alternative suggestions have been put forward. One member of the Force proposed that private detectives should be controlled in the nature of the activities they pursue, that is, limited to those concerning divorce, the tracing of relatives, the services of legal processes, character enquiries concerning future employees, credit-rating and debt collecting, and taking statements for solicitors. The article, which appeared in the May 1972 edition of the *Police Review*, went on to say that private detectives should be prohibited from pursuing political enquiries, enquiries from foreign powers, any assignment involving 'bugging', and matters subject to police investigation. The Association of British Investigators, although agreeing with the first three stipulations, reacted strongly against the last on the grounds that the police are often too busy collecting evidence for the prosecution to gather all the evidence which might be useful to the defence. This is obviously a valid argument and one to which the majority of police are not blind. A Superintendent in the Force put the other side of the argument this way, 'A defence is often put forward as a result of an independent private investigation. To suggest that there should be a prohibition would mean that there could never be an investigation by an independent source.' He concluded, 'No doubt you see the dangers.'

The dangers to which this policeman is referring can be well illustrated by several cases in which private detectives have produced evidence which has led to the release from prison of a person wrongly convicted of a crime. In America in 1973, for example, a man was released from prison after serving eighteen years for murder. A private detective, Lee Walker, who had maintained the man's innocence from the beginning, took on the case without charge and personally posted a bond of $5,000 for a new trial. The man was acquitted. More recently, in this country, a Humberside private investigator, Bernard Rayner, took on a similar case. The victim in this instance had served several years of a prison sentence before Mr Rayner, who had been employed by the man's father, gathered together enough evidence to prove the son's innocence and secure his release. The resultant legal costs to the father ran into thousands of pounds, but were private detectives to be excluded from doing work of this nature the consequences would obviously be serious. Trying to stifle the activities of private investigators is a negative approach.

There is also controversy within the police force over certain operations of security firms. In 1970, Inspector Reg Gale, the chairman of the Police Federation, said:

It should not be necessary for any company to do some of the things they are doing now; some of the duties are a police function. I'm not suggesting we want to do a night watchman's job, wandering around testing door locks. I'm not suggesting that we want to do the pay side that some of the larger firms do. But I have felt that the guarding of large sums of money or bullion is a police job and we can undertake it. [Reported in the *Private Investigator*, August 1970.]

It is some years since Inspector Gale made these assertions. One wonders whether he would be so certain now that the police could undertake such work. There is no doubt that many of his colleagues, especially in Metropolitan areas, do not share this view. Security companies, themselves, have a tendency to insist that none of the work they do is properly a police job, but we have already seen a few of the borderline operations carried out by some firms. Moreover, *The Times* of 19 August 1974 reported the director of a well-known security company as saying, 'The police can only give a general protection to the community; sooner or later private firms will move into any area not covered by the police where there is a need and a profit.' There are certainly occasions on which the use or contemplated use of private police is directly attributable to the failure of the regular police to control crime.

The Business *Observer* of 6 December 1970 reported on a situation in Derby that had forced local traders to consider hiring private guards. Burglaries of shops had become so frequent that the local Chamber of Trade felt it had to take some security measures itself, as the police, 300 men under-strength, were having no success. In the end the scheme was abandoned because of the difficulty of employing suitable men for the job. But at the time when it seemed as though the scheme would go ahead the chief constable of the region commented in the journal *Police*, 'There can be no question that I have delegated my responsibility to private security organizations but it would be wholly wrong of me to deny the members of the local Chamber of Trade the right to protect themselves whilst at the same time telling them that I cannot deploy the officers required to provide the services they and we would wish.'

Six years later a similar situation arose in Kent, and the *Sevenoaks Chronicle* outlined the propositions that the victims, in this case several companies on an industrial estate, had put forward to counter the criminals:

A plan to beat the week-end raiders who persistently break into firms on the Vestry industrial estate has been applauded by Sevenoaks police ... Detective Inspector Ivor Moore, head of the Sevenoaks CID said, 'This is a good idea and could help us. We do patrol the estate but obviously the amount of times we can patrol during the night are limited due to callouts that we get for other disturbances and our lack of manpower.'

In both the cases cited here, the police were sympathetic towards the individuals who felt that they would like to provide themselves with private security to supplement that of the police. But at other times it has been suggested that the police fear competition from security firms, and that it is this fear which leads them to oppose a licensing system. My own view is that this allegation is groundless. It is true that in America, where 'moonlighting' for private employers to get extra money is quite common among regular policemen, quite a serious state of competition has arisen. But there seems to be very little evidence to support a similar contention here. Although policemen are available for private hire, the jobs that they do in this country, such as policing football matches and other public events, should not fall within the scope of the private sector.

There have, however, been suggestions from within police ranks, notable from Mr George Terry, the chief constable of Sussex, that the police should have their own commercial security branch. Similar schemes do operate in other countries – Singapore, for example, has a Government-run security agency – but for the moment, at least, such a suggestion seems purely academic until the police force can recruit enough men to fulfil its present needs. In addition there is evidence that there would be strong opposition to such a plan from within the private sector.

Any conflict that exists between private and public police seems, therefore, to occur in situations where their respective functions become blurred and confused. Confusion may arise, not only in relation to the activities of the two bodies, but also in relation to their physical appearance. Security companies and private detectives have always maintained that the last thing they want is to be confused in the minds of the public with regular policemen; indeed. IPSA's recent change in name was a deliberate move to prevent any unfortunate association. But this is a consideration that has weighed heavily with the police and authorities in relation to licensing.

It was seen in the last chapter that bodies submitting evidence to the Younger Committee on the subject of private investigators expressed concern at the possible misrepresentations that might occur were they to be issued with identity cards, probably with photographs, resembling those of the police. In fact the problem is already with us. Members of the Association of British Investigators, for example, are given identity cards to prove the membership of the holder and, although they are not very similar to police warrant cards, to the uninitiated they might be mistaken as such. Indeed, although members would not positively represent themselves as policemen, one or two have admitted to using their identity card in order to try to obtain co-operation from members of the public in the course of an investigation. There can be no doubt that on occasion the citizen is left with the impression that the private detective had some right to his co-operation.

As far as security companies are concerned, similar confusion results from the uniform-clad appearance of their guards. The companies say that this practice simply identifies their employees, creates an efficient image and advertises their enterprise. Is there, however, more to a guard's uniform than this? Is it trying to put forward the impression of an ostensible authority that the 'officer' does not in fact possess? Many companies also organize their employees in ranks of security guard, sergeant, inspector, etc. Are they trying to emphasize the 'police force image' in order to obtain more co-operation from the public? The security companies themselves give a categorical 'no' to these questions. Securicor states that the blue and white uniforms of its men are specifically designed to avoid confusion with the police, and Group 4 is likewise insistent that its livery is unmistakable (although it is in the process of changing it from blue to grey to dispel all doubts). Nevertheless, one cannot help but feel that security firms are optimistic in the measure of discernment they attribute to the public.

In America, the authorities have taken a more positive line against the tendency of companies to simulate official law-enforcement agencies. A model statute drafted by the Private Security Advisory Council provides, in relation to uniform and equipment:

(a) No individual, while performing the duties of an armed or unarmed private security officer shall wear or display any badge, insignia, device, shield, patch or pattern which shall indicate that he is a sworn peace officer or which contains or includes the word 'police' or the equivalent thereof or is similar in wording to any law enforcement agency in this State; . . .

(c) If a private security officer is required to wear a uniform, it shall be furnished by the employer. All military or police-style uniforms shall, except for rainwear or other foul weather clothing, have:

(1) affixed over the left breast pocket, on the outermost garment and on all caps worn by such persons, badges distinct in design from

those utilized by law enforcement agencies within the State, and approved by the licensing authority;

(2) affixed over the right breast pocket of such outermost garment a plate or tape of the size 5″ × 1″ with the words 'security officer'.

The Government report to which the statute is annexed goes further and proposes that all private security uniforms should be of a colour designated by the State and different from law-enforcement colours. A similar stipulation is already embodied in Sweden's new law, and Bruce George, too, has intimated that he hopes to include regulations on uniform and appearance in his Bill.

The relationship between public and private police can be seen to be an uncertain and somewhat difficult one, and this uneasiness may well increase as the private sector inevitably grows in proportion to the regular police force. Some insight into the future development of that relationship can perhaps be gained by looking at the present situation in America, although naturally too close a comparison is dangerous. The 1977 Report on the Security Industry finds that there is friction between private security and law-enforcement agencies due, among other things, to lack of mutual respect, lack of co-operation, lack of communication, lack of knowledge about private security on the part of the police, and the failure of the security industry to speak with a unified voice. These are all observations that could apply in this country. The Report called for a closer working relationship between the two bodies, through co-operation and the interchange of information. It recommends, in effect, that the security industry should, indeed must, be treated as a partner in crime prevention. The Report concludes: 'The application of the resources, technology, skills and knowledge of the private security industry presents the best hope available for protecting the citizen who has witnessed his defences against crime shrink to a level which leaves him virtually unprotected.'

The situation in this country is not yet so serious, but there is no sign of a slowing-down in the crime rate. Alarms, safes, locks and electronic equipment have already achieved an accepted place in crime prevention. The position of the human element is less certain. This is due chiefly to the ambiguous stance adopted by the Home Office on this question. Its advisers have occupied a 'half-way house' in their attitude to the industry – forced to recognize the need for private security resources, and yet unwilling to take the responsibility to increase their efficiency. 'Private police' can never achieve full acceptability in their present position because, at the moment, it is difficult to know whether there is more danger in the threat of crime or in the employment, in a security role, of unqualified, untrained and unchecked individuals.

The police are still walking on that tight-rope over the question of co-operation with their private counterparts, but security and detective firms are themselves walking on a far narrower line. One senior police officer was reported in the *Observer* of 2 September 1973 as saying of the large security organizations who claim that their employees are rigorously vetted, 'We do not see how this can be done without access to police records and any such access gained unlawfully must be highly improper.' It seems to be a case, on the part of some police officers, of 'heads we win, tails you lose'.

Conclusion

If there is one feature which characterizes the security and detective professions, it is the fact that their members are people of extraordinarily strong personality and conviction. If there is another such feature, it is that practically every person with experience in the field takes a different view either of the concept of security as a whole, or of a particular aspect of the business, be it arming, licensing or personnel selection. The real professionals in the industry are, by and large, knowledgeable and interesting, but above all, they are persuasive speakers and debaters.

The result of these factors combined is that within the security and detective world, a controversial area in itself, there is a clash of theories and ideas among its practitioners which is almost without parallel in other industries. Many of the leading figures are personal friends, but their views on the work in which they are involved are often fundamentally different.

This variety and strength of personalities adds immense colour to the security industry, but it certainly does not help in the search for a solution to problems which can only be resolved through united thought.

One thing is beyond doubt. The intrusion of private security forces into the fabric of our modern society can no longer be ignored, and the consequences of this intrusion must no longer be swept under the carpet. Whether we like it or not, the reality of the situation is that the private sector occupies an increasing role in crime prevention. This must be recognized by the authorities, and they should act accordingly.

The biggest danger of the present situation is not, in my view, the possibility of persons with criminal records infiltrating the industry, although this is, not surprisingly, the aspect which receives the most publicity, and is indeed very worrying. No, the real threat lies in the incidence of poor-quality services and inadequate training and instruction in what now constitutes a second-string police force in this country.

Measures must be taken, and taken soon, to ensure a high standard among the firms that are now relieving in part the burden on an overworked and undermanned police force. This must be done if we are to preserve, in this country, a tradition of good law enforcement, and if the high reputation of our police force is to be passed on to, and upheld by, the new generation of crime-prevention officers – the new 'private police'.

Index

More about Penguins and Pelicans

Penguinews, which appears every month, contains details of all the new books issued by Penguins as they are published. It is supplemented by our stocklist, which includes around 5,000 titles.

A specimen copy of *Penguinews* will be sent to you free on request. Please write to Dept EP, Penguin Books Ltd, Harmondsworth, Middlesex, for your copy.

In the U.S.A.: For a complete list of books available from Penguins in the United States write to Dept CS, Penguin Books, 625 Madison Avenue, New York, New York 10022.

In Canada: For a complete list of books available from Penguins in Canada write to Penguin Books Canada Ltd, 2801 John Street, Markham, Ontario L3R 1B4

Beyond the Limits of the Law

Tom Bowden

Do you regard your local policeman as a friendly bobby, or armed tyrant? Is he there to guard, guide and help, or as the watchdog of a strong government? The answers to these questions depend very much on where you live, and yet the images are not quite so far apart as we sometimes think.

Police are asked to do the impossible: as fellow citizens they are employed by the state to ensure that the state is not subverted either by crime or by certain types of political activity. *Beyond the Limits of the Law* examines the way in which police maintain law and order, while at the same time being subject to it. Tom Bowden has written a sympathetic and comparative study which analyses a number of extreme situations (taking his examples from America, China and France as well as Britain) where the role of the policeman has been put to the test. In each instance, precisely because he has been in the hottest spot, he has acted beyond the law, and in doing so, raised fundamental questions.

Quis custodiet ipsos custodes? Who watches the watchdogs?